Praise for *Angry Women*

"DR. MCCLURE'S EXCELLENT BOOK is a must-read for every woman. We all have problems with anger—sometimes our own, and sometimes someone else's. This book offers very specific and easy-to-use techniques that help us take control of our own anger and avoid being controlled by others' anger. So, bypass 'Don't get mad, get even' and, instead, listen to Dr. McClure: 'Go ahead and get mad, but take control and come out ahead'."

—**Dr. Alexis Artwohl**, Survival Triangle Training, pyschologist and law enforcement trainer; www.alexisartwohl.com

"WHETHER YOU READ THIS BOOK in one sitting or in a couple of days, its instan   rest of your life—for   own anger in way   w to stop being   nore control ove   "

—**L**   *the Warrior*   )ave .com

By Lynne McClure, Ph.D.

Angry Women: Stop Letting Anger Control Your Life

Angry Men: Managing Anger in an Unforgiving World

Anger & Conflict in the Workplace: Spot the Signs, Avoid the Trauma

Risky Business: Managing Employee Violence in the Workplace

Managing High-Risk Behaviors (video)

ANGRY WOMEN
STOP LETTING ANGER CONTROL YOUR LIFE!

LYNNE McCLURE, PH.D.

Impact Publications
Manassas, VA

ISBN: 1-57023-206-7

Library of Congress: 2003103455

Publisher: For information on Impact Publications, including current and forth-coming publications, authors, press kits, online bookstore, and submission requirements, visit our website: www.impactpublications.com

Publicity/Rights: For information on publicity, author interviews, and subsidiary rights, contact the Media Relations Department: Tel. 703-361-7300, Fax 703-335-9486, or email: info@impactpublications.com.

Sales/Distribution: All bookstore sales are handled through Impact's trade distributor: National Book Network, 15200 NBN Way, Blue Ridge Summit, PA 17214, Tel. 1-800-4626420. All other sales and distribution inquiries should be directed to the publisher: Sales Department, IMPACT PUBLICATIONS, 9104 Manassas Drive, Suite N, Manassas Park, VA 20111-5211, Tel. 703-361-7300, Fax 703-335-9486, or email: info@impactpublications.com.

Layout and Design by Donna B. McGreevy.

Contents

Dedication   viii

Acknowledgments   ix

Foreword   xi

Does Anger Control You?   1

1   The Many Faces of Anger   5
- Jealousy can lead to anger—and so can feeling trapped   6
- Sometimes anger comes from having no control over what happens to you and your body   7
- Being questioned can make you angry   8
- Anger can come from date-rape   9
- Sometimes, having to be strong can make you angry   10
- Wanting something can make you angry   11
- Unfairness at work can make you angry   11
- You may get angry at your kids   12
- This may surprise you, but grief can make you angry   13
- Domestic violence can make you angry   14
- Giving up addictions can bring out your anger   15
- Incest can make you angry   16
- And pornography can make you angry— in two different ways   17

2   Take Charge of Your Own Anger   20
- What You Feel and What You Do   20
- How to Make S-P-A-C-E Between What You Feel and What You Do   23

3   Seven Ways Other People Use Their Anger to Control You   25
- 1. Acted-Out Anger   25
- 2. Irresponsible Anger   27
- 3. Self-Centered Anger   28
- 4. Two-Faced Anger   29

      5. Rigid Anger   31

      6. Drinking/Drugging Anger   32

      7. Delusional Anger   33

4   Decide Whether to Talk Now—When You're Angry   37

5   Talk to the Right Person—When You're Angry   40
    ■   What to Do   40
    ■   How to Do It   41

6   Pay Attention to Their Feelings—When You're Angry   44
    ■   More About What You Say and How You Say It   45
    ■   Checklist   49

7   Find Something in Common—When You're Angry   50

8   Depersonalize the Situation—When You're Angry   53
    ■   How to Not Take Things Personally   54
    ■   How to Talk in a Depersonalized Way   55

9   Get to the Real Issue(s)—When You're Angry   59
    ■   The Real Issue   59
    ■   How to Talk About the Real Issue   61
    ■   Sometimes the Real Issue Changes   63
    ■   After You've Discussed the Real Issue—If They're
        Working With You   65

10 Drop the Grudge—When You're Angry   67
    ■   How to Drop the Grudge So You Can Act Now   67
    ■   Letting Go of Grudges in General   68
    ■   How to Drop the Grudge When the Other
        Person Wants to Get You   71
    ■   Grieving   72

11 Applying the Seven Skills to Our Opening Stories   75
    ■   Jealousy   76
    ■   No control over what happens to you   80
    ■   Being questioned   84
    ■   Date-raped   88
    ■   Having to be strong   92
    ■   Wanting something   95

- ■ Unfairness at work 97
- ■ Your kids 99
- ■ Grief 102
- ■ Domestic violence 104
- ■ How to Interview a Therapist or Helper 108
- ■ Giving up addictions 109
- ■ Incest 112
- ■ Pornography 115
- ■ Putting You—Not Anger—in Control of Your Life 118

The Author 119
Index 121
Career Resources 125

Dedication

To

Tanya Lynne Yoakum,
the only woman I know who has
no issues with anger or control...

And to all women who do

.

Acknowledgments

This book came from the experience, and help, of a lot of people. I want to thank each one.

First is Dr. Judith Reisman, my friend and dedicated champion of women and healthy relationships, for support "beyond the call of duty."

To every woman in prison, at home, and at work who shared her story about being controlled by her *own*—or someone *else's*—anger. The need for privacy prevents me from listing your names, but you each know who you are.

To Ron Krannich, my publisher, a man of vision who saw the need, believed in my work, and suggested the book. To Mardie Younglof, my editor, whose flexibility made everything possible. And to Barry Littmann, whose artwork shines on the cover.

To all my family and friends, who are more patient than one should reasonably expect.

To my parents, who taught me to love books and believe in people.

To my clients, students, and workshop participants, who truly are my teachers.

And to everyone else who tries to make things a little better—my heartfelt thanks.

—Lynne McClure, Ph.D.

Foreword

As an expert in the behavioral field, Dr. Lynne McClure knows all too well the risks of relying constantly on "experts" instead of on our own common sense.

I agree with the basic premise of this book—that you need to trust yourself, your feelings, and your own view of your experiences. The goal is to *help* you—while you help *yourself*. Dr. McClure will serve as a trusty field guide.

She aims to open up some easier paths in your emotional forest – paths that she has seen before. She will help clear away some of the fallen debris, showing you how to move some of the stumbling blocks out of your way.

But this is *your* exploration. *You* will choose your direction. *You* will decide just where you really want to go. As Dr. McClure says, the "experts" have, for too long, undermined women's faith in their own opinions, sense of self, righteousness, honor, and dignity. "Trust yourself" is her motto.

I think you will find, in this easy-to-read book, the strength and support you need for your birthright of nobility and valor.

—***Dr. Judith Reisman,*** world-renowned expert
on domestic violence and child abuse.
Author of *Soft Porn Plays Hardball; Kinsey,
Crimes,& Consequences;* and many other
books and papers

ANGRY WOMEN

Does Anger Control You?

How many of these apply to you? Check each one that does:

1. You come across as strong and independent—but inside you feel unsure of yourself. _____

2. You come across as passive and quiet. _____

3. You pick men who are bad for you. _____

4. You have a love-hate relationship with food. _____

5. Your life is very stressful. _____

6. You feel tired a lot. _____

7. You've had sex with lots of different men. _____

8. One or more men or women in your life have hit you, beaten you, or hurt you physically in other ways. _____

9. You do everything you can to avoid conflict. _____

10. You're lonely—even when you're with people you love. _____

11. One or more men or women in your life have played "mind-games" with you. _____

12. You *over*eat, or *refuse* to eat, when you're stressed. _____

13. You use alcohol and/or "recreational" drugs to relax. _____

14. You often feel depressed. _____

15. You have fears that don't make sense to others. _____

16. You pretend to be happier than you are.   _____

17. You've been raped and/or molested.   _____

18. You take prescription drugs for anxiety, depression, or sleeping problems.   _____

19. You've been put down, criticized, and/or told you were no good, by men and/or women.   _____

20. When you're angry, you *don't* talk about it.   _____

21. You have chronic fatigue, lupus, fibromyalgia, asthma, or other auto-immune health conditions.   _____

22. Sometimes you're angry but don't even know it.   _____

23. You have an eating disorder.   _____

24. You were sexually molested (or abused in other ways) as a child—or you have a *feeling* that you were.   _____

25. The family you grew up in has secrets or "skeletons in the closet."   _____

26. You cry easily.   _____

27. You have kids from more than one man.   _____

28. You think you might have been date-raped, where date-rape drugs were used.   _____

29. You've cut yourself or done other things to hurt yourself physically.   _____

30. When you get a new boyfriend, he turns out to be more like the old ones than you thought he'd be.   _____

31. When you get angry, you feel depressed.   _____

32. You're afraid of your current man and/or your ex.   _____

33. You feel like you can't take care of yourself.   _____

34. You've tried to kill yourself, or had moments when
    suicide appealed to you.   _____

The more of these you checked, the more you need this book—and the more this book will help you.

If you're in a relationship right now with someone who beats you, go directly to pages 63-65 and pages 104-109. When you're safe, come back to this page. The whole book will be helpful to you.

Anger is *not* the "only" reason behind the items on this list. But anger is a *big part* of them. Even when you *don't know* you're angry.

You can get trapped by your own anger. You may deny it, hide it, and talk yourself out of it. You may take it out on yourself—and hurt both yourself and the people you love, by doing this. You may actively hurt others when you're angry. You may let anger hurt your self-image, narrow your choices, limit your career, and destroy your family. You may let anger lead you into depression, eating disorders, and destructive relationships.

Your anger may lead you to alcohol and drugs. Stealing. Shoplifting. Prostitution. Even murder. Your anger may have led—or may lead—you to prison.

One of the problems is that women are *raised* to be controlled. You may feel controlled by other people's needs. You may have been taught to take care of everyone *but* yourself. To smile no matter how mad you feel. To keep your anger to yourself. To make sure everyone "gets along"—no matter what kind of toll this takes on *you*.

You may have been taught to be controlled by those around you. Your man. Your kids. Your boss. TV ads. Media images of women. Porn. Food. Alcohol. Drugs. Men. Other women.

Maybe you're controlled by *other people's* anger. So-called "partners" who beat you. Threaten you. Emotionally and mentally abuse you. Men *or* women who play on your fears to get you to do what *they* want.

Your man's anger may have turned you into a *captive*. A prisoner in your own home. Maybe you had to cover up about the fact that he hit you. Maybe you lied about other things, to protect him. Refused to say what you knew about a theft, a drug deal, a murder. You may have put up with a lot of bad things someone did—to you or to others—when they were angry.

Whether it's other people's or your own, you've learned to let anger control *you* and *your life*.

This fact is enough to make you *really* angry.

This book will show you how to take—or take *back*—control of your life. You'll identify with the real-life examples of how anger takes over. By the time you finish this book, you'll know how to *stop* letting anger—your own, or someone else's—control you.

And you'll know how to get back your *life.*

We'll start with real stories from real women like yourself. See how many of the stories relate to you. The details will be different—but the feelings may be the same.

After the stories, you'll get the skills to handle your *own—and others'*—anger. In the last part of the book, we'll apply all these skills to the stories.

You'll learn how to stop letting anger control your life. And how to put your life back in *your own* hands.

1

The Many Faces of Anger

Anger shows many different faces. They may not even look like anger. See how many of them relate to you.

- Jealousy can lead to anger—and so can feeling trapped
- Sometimes anger comes from having no control over what happens to you and your body
- Being questioned can make you angry
- Anger can come from date-rape
- Sometimes, having to be strong can make you angry
- Wanting something can make you angry
- Unfairness at work can make you angry
- You may get angry at your kids
- This may surprise you, but grief can make you angry
- Domestic violence can make you angry
- Giving up addictions can bring out your anger
- Incest can make you angry
- And pornography can make you angry— in two different ways

Jealousy can lead to anger—and so can feeling trapped

I knew he was going out on me. He denied it, but I knew. You know how you just know stuff like that? The more he said he wasn't, the more sure I was that he was.

But here's the thing. I work all day. I have no time to chase him around to see who he's with or what he's doing. When I get home, there's the kids to take care of. I can't track him down when he says he's out with his buddies.

So I have no proof. At least, none that I can show him. But he's been staying out later than usual. He doesn't push me for sex like he used to. He suddenly decides one day that he should take care of the checkbook instead of me.

And you know what else? He's gotten a lot nicer. To me. I know this sounds crazy, but that's what really proves it to me. He's nicer because he's guilty.

So I'm angry. Real angry. What does he think I am, his maid? Not thin enough? Not young enough? Not sexy enough? Who can be sexy with three kids and a lot of bills? That jerk thinks I'm too stupid to catch on. He thinks he can go out on me and get away with it. I'm angry enough to divorce him.

But there's the kids. He makes a lot more money than me. I'd have to get a cheaper place to live. One month of him skipping child support, and the kids and I would be out in the street.

And then there's custody. The kids are close to him. He could afford to stay here and keep the kids in the same school. I could lose the kids if I divorced him.

And if I did get custody, or even if I just left, the kids would hate my guts. They'd blame me for breaking up the family.

So, yeah, I'm angry. And you know what I do about it? Nothing. I smile, act the same as always. I act like nothing's wrong. You know why? Because it's easier for everyone that way.

That's why I like the Valium so much. It takes the edge off. It helps me get through the day.

Sometimes anger comes from having no control over what happens to you and your body

Nobody understands this. Not even my doctor. Food makes me sick to my stomach. The sight of it. The way it looks. The way it smells. But the worst part is the feel of it in my mouth. It makes me gag.

I've never told this to anyone before. It makes me gag to even say it.

But the feel of food in my mouth is just like when I was little. The babysitter stuck something in my mouth. I was terrified. I felt like I was suffocating. Drowning. The slimy feel in my mouth and throat.

I had no idea at the time what was happening. I didn't have the words to even know what I felt. Now I can say I felt terrified. But I also felt dirty. Ashamed. Disgusted. He had done a disgusting thing to me. I was too little to know what was going on. But I felt all these ways.

And that's what food feels like. Every time I put food in my mouth, it feels like that. Even the smell of food does it to me.

Everyone tries to get me to eat. Some come straight out and tell me to eat. Others are sneakier. They ask if I'm hungry, or they eat something and look at me as if I'll get hungry from watching.

Or they'll lecture me about all the dangers of not eating. How all my organs will shut down. My guts, my liver, my kidneys. My doctor does this. But he doesn't understand. Talking about my organs does the same thing as the food. It all makes me feel like throwing up.

It all makes me mad. I get angry at the way they think they can talk me into wanting to eat. Like I'm still a child. I get angry that they don't even know how I feel. I get mad at myself for not being able to tell them.

Anyway, I found a way to get my mind off the whole subject. I work out—as many hours a day as I can.

Being questioned can make you angry

Sometimes my boyfriend makes me so mad. Things will be just fine, and then, bam! He starts asking me all these questions.

Today, I get home from work, and right away he wants to know if Rick, a guy I work with, was there today. That made me mad.

What difference does it make whether Rick was there or not? He's just one of my co-workers. He's this computer nerd, and my boyfriend knows it. So I asked him why he wanted to know.

Well, that set him right off. He starts yelling about me keeping secrets from him. He goes on and on, saying stuff about me liking Rick, sneaking out with him for lunch, stuff like that. I finally told him yes, Rick was there. So then he goes, "See? And how come you asked why I wanted to know? I have a right to know which guys you're hanging out with!"

It didn't do any good to remind him that Rick is just another guy I work with. Or that I'm working, not hanging out. I reminded him that Rick is just a computer nerd. That still didn't do any good. He wanted to know where I had lunch, who was there, stuff like that. He just went on and on.

I was so mad! But it doesn't do any good to tell him that. He just gets louder and has more questions. I felt like slapping him in the face and walking out.

But I did what I always do when he gets like this. I told him no man could measure up to him. I rubbed up against him. We wound up having sex.

Which made me even angrier.

Anger can come from date-rape

I would never have believed this could happen to me. But there I was, at a party with a bunch of my friends, and the next thing I know, I wake up in a strange room. I'm alone in some strange bed, and I've peed all over myself. My head feels weird, like I'm in a fog or a dream. My clothes are all over the floor. At the time, I didn't even think about my car—which, it turned out, was still at my friend's house where the party was.

I was terrified. I didn't even know where I was. Nothing looked familiar. I couldn't think clearly. I couldn't remember anyone's phone number. I got more and more afraid by the minute. My heart was pounding and racing. My head was so fuzzy. My whole crotch area really, really hurt.

I was scared. Then I realized I'd been raped. I vomited. I felt sick. I wanted to crawl right out of my body. I felt dirty, filthy. I threw up again.

I took a shower. Wanted to wash everything off of me. Over and over. Wanted to shower to make me clean, clean, clean. Maybe it would also clear my head. I got dressed. Then I realized I should call the police.

It turns out I was only a few miles from where I live. A neighborhood I'd never been in before. I'd been drugged—one of those date-rape drugs. Never tasted anything. Never saw or smelled anything. Can't remember anything after talking to a bunch of people at the party.

I'd been raped, all right. Sodomized, too. God knows by who, or how many guys, or how many times. Thank God I didn't get pregnant, on top of everything else. No signs of STD. At least, not so far.

But the shower had washed away the evidence. No way to prove who'd done what. Even my friends could only guess. They were all so drunk or high or stoned at the party that no one remembered when I left or who with.

I can't even tell you whether I'm angry. I understand what happened. I know it's not my fault. I know I should be angry.

But I don't feel angry. What I feel like is . . . well, I feel like a piece of dirt. Like no matter how many showers I take, nothing will ever make me clean. I feel dirty all over.

I dream about it every night. One dream I have over and over—I'm in the shower, and so much water washes over me that I dissolve, just disappear, right there in the shower. All gone, along with the dirt.

But I can't say I'm angry. I'm just a lot more private now. More careful about who I talk to and where I go. And I stay away from parties.

Sometimes, having to be strong can make you angry

I left home when I was 12. Couldn't get along with my folks. My father kept trying to control my life, and my mother just followed whatever he said. He wanted me to be like her—no guts, no backbone, no life of her own. She was just a servant to him.

I think now that I was too strong for my father. He knew he couldn't control me. I even stood up to him when I was five and he tried to touch me wrong. I told him I'd tell the police if he tried again. Five years old! I had to be strong, with the way things were at home.

So when I left, some friends said I could stay at their houses. But the parents always kicked me out for no reason at all. After a while, I got real angry about having to count on other people. It was too much like living with my parents.

So that's how I decided to work the streets. Easy money. Not hard work, like cleaning people's houses. I wasn't like some of the other girls, who got talked into it, or got forced into it. I made the decision myself.

I also knew I didn't need no guy to protect me. I could take care of myself. And, for a while, it worked. But some of the customers were scary. One guy punched me so hard he knocked a tooth out. Another beat me with the handle of his gun, for no reason at all.

So then this fancy guy tells me I'll be dead if I don't have a man to protect me. I knew he was right. So I let him do that for me. And he was real nice to me. For a while.

But it turned out I was just another one of the girls to him. He was just another guy trying to control me.

But it don't do no good to get angry, you know. He don't care. My customers don't care. Even I don't care! I just light up or shoot or smoke or whatever's around.

And then I'm not so angry for a while.

Wanting something can make you angry

I didn't start out walking into a store for the purpose of stealing. One day, there I was, getting a pack of cigarettes. While the cashier was breaking a roll of coins, I saw this glittery thing. It was a little change purse, hanging on a hook. It was just there. So I grabbed it and folded it up in my free hand.

She didn't see. I paid for my cigarettes and left.

The next time, I was in a bigger store, and there was this loose pile of underwear. I grabbed a few panties and stuffed them in my shirt.

After a while, I'd picked up enough clothes to have a whole new wardrobe. All for free!

And you know, I deserve these things. Other people have the money to buy stuff. It's not my fault that I don't. I didn't have any rich parents to buy me nice things. I don't have any rich boyfriend, either.

And when you see what kinds of crooks are running the companies, why should I pay for anything? They have more money than I do. And everyone else I know.

So I don't really think of it as stealing. It's more like, you know, just getting what I need. So when I end up in jail, it makes me furious. How come everyone else can get away with it, but not me?

Unfairness at work can make you angry

I've had this job for three years now. My boss knows I do a good job.

But this new woman starts working there, and for some reason she starts bad-mouthing me. She tells everyone that I just slack off when I should be working. Who does she think she is? She really made me mad.

But the next thing I know, my boss calls me in. He starts asking me questions about how I'm spending my time, whether there's a way to get more done in the same amount of time, things like that. I know that's because of what this new woman has been saying.

Why does my boss believe her, when I'm the one who's been doing a good job for three years? It makes me furious!

You may get angry at your kids

My boy had just turned two. I couldn't let him out of my sight for three seconds. He opens everything up, tries to drink out of any cups or glasses he can reach, and keeps turning on the water faucet. He loves to play with electric outlets, and when I smack his hand and tell him "no," he just laughs and runs away.

One day, when I'm sick with the flu, he climbs up on the entertainment center, gets on top of the TV, and tries to push the TV to the floor. If I hadn't come running in right then, he could've ended up with the TV on top of him.

I'd had enough! I grabbed him, and he's so strong that he's hanging onto the TV. I had trouble pulling him off. I was afraid the damn thing would fall on both of us. The whole time, he's yelling, "No! No!" It was like my whole purpose in life was to watch after him!

I was sick, my head was pounding, and I was afraid the TV would hurt him. But I was also angry. SO angry that I just started hitting him. I couldn't stop. I heard him screaming, "Stop, Mama! Stop, Mama!" I was so mad I couldn't stop myself.

His little voice sounded so far away. I was furious. I hit him and kept hitting, hitting. I hit him until he suddenly got quiet.

Real quiet.

This may surprise you, but grief can make you angry

When my grandmother died, I was so sad I couldn't even cry. I was 12 years old.

She was the one who really raised me. She lived with me and my mother and my older sisters and brothers. But my mother worked, and when she was home she was always yelling at one of us. Everybody else was busy doing stuff, and Grandma was the only one I could talk to.

She'd read to me and tell me stories about when she was a little girl. When I got older and started my period, it was Grandma who told me about sex. Even when I had my first boyfriend and I wanted to hide everything from my mother, I told Grandma. I loved her, and I knew she loved me.

I was shocked at my own reaction when she died. I couldn't cry, not for a long time. But I got mad—angry at her for dying! How could she do this to me? I even felt ashamed for being angry. I thought how selfish I was, worrying about myself when Grandma's the one who died. But I was angry for days.

Finally, I broke down and cried. Cried and cried. Sad as I was, it felt better than being angry at her.

Domestic violence can make you angry

I'm more afraid of him than in love with him.

I probably loved him at the beginning. He was always so sweet to me when we were dating. He paid more attention to me than any guy ever had.

But slowly, just a little bit at a time, he started finding fault with me. I was too fat, or too short, or too loud. He'd always find something. When it hurt my feelings, he'd say he was just joking. When he yelled, it was clear that he really felt that way.

I can see it now, looking back. But I didn't see it then. One by one, he made me get rid of all my friends. Each time, he had a good reason— good in his mind, that is. I got so lost in each example that I didn't see what was happening until later. Two, maybe three, years after we were married, I had no friends left.

He'd already started hitting me by then. It was because I did something stupid. Or looked at him wrong. Or was too fat or ugly. Then he started hitting me because he "knew" I had another man. Ha! I was already like a prisoner in my own house by then. Who could go find another man? And feeling so bad about myself, what man would want me anyway?

Then he started in on my family. Again, one by one. This cousin didn't like him, so it was bad for me to see her. Then another cousin. Then he got to my sister and my brothers. The last was my own mother. I can't believe I did it, looking back. But one by one, I gave up everyone close to me, for him.

Sometimes, when he'd hit me, he would cry with me and swear he'd never do it again. I believed him. I was so stupid! I believed him every time, even though he always hit me again. I was so afraid of him that I never even asked what made him do it.

Other times, he be in a rage and blame me. He said he really didn't want to hit me, but he knew I was lying to him, so it was my fault. Every time he hit me, he had a different excuse.

Sometimes, he'd hit me so hard I'd get a black eye. Other times, he'd hit my head against the wall and I'd feel really dizzy for a long time. He yelled that I deserved this because of how cheap my clothes made me look.

I always said I was sorry. But he'd always hit me again.

Now he hits me every time something goes wrong. It might be something I did, or something he thinks I did. It might be something that has nothing to do with me.

And he doesn't promise anymore that it won't happen again. Instead, he says it's my fault and I deserve it. And he says he'll kill me if I even think about leaving him.

I'm angry at him for what he does to me. I'm also terrified of him. But I'm also angry at myself. How did I let this happen?

Giving up addictions can bring out your anger

I knew for a long time that I smoked and drank too much. Did drugs too much. I even quit a few times. But not for long.

At first, it felt so powerful to quit. Every time. Like I was on top of things, I could handle it. Kind of like a high in itself.

And fighting the urge, that felt powerful too. Even the headaches and the sleepless nights felt like just a test at first. A challenge.

But here's what got me every time. My moods. I got real moody, real sensitive, every time I quit. Everyone got on my nerves. Everything they did bothered me.

I got angry real easy. And real fast. I even got afraid of my anger. I wanted to tell everybody off. I wanted to hit them, beat them up. I got angry at anything anyone did or said. I yelled a lot.

I was shocked. This wasn't like me. I never got this way when I smoked or did drugs or drank. I was afraid of myself. I was afraid of my own anger. I was afraid of what I might do.

It was easier to go back to smoking, drinking, drugging.

Incest can make you angry

My father started molesting me when I was about four. He'd do it while my mother was out doing her friends' hair and he was supposed to be babysitting me. He'd bring me to his bed and fondle me. I don't remember everything he did to me.

When I turned 12 and got my period, I told him to stop or I'd tell my mother on him. It took me all those years before I had the guts to say that to him. He stopped.

I can't believe my mother didn't know. I can't believe she didn't see how I couldn't look her in the eye. How I didn't want to be near him at all. How I cried when she left to do her friends' hair. When I was little, I thought she could tell how I felt inside. I felt sick, scared, and angry. I felt ashamed. I felt guilty. I felt very, very alone. I felt afraid of my own father.

It took me a few years to tell her about it. I was 15. She asked why I was so rude to him. Why I refused to go anywhere with the two of them. So I told her.

At first, she didn't believe me. That made me furious. But I felt too guilty and ashamed, maybe even afraid, to get mad at her. I just kept telling her the same thing, over and over.

Finally, one day, she said she believed me. I started to feel this immense relief all over my body. I felt like a big sigh of relief was finally coming out of me. I felt like she would do something to make it right. Get him arrested. Divorce him. Make him see how he'd hurt me. And her.

Instead, she was real quiet for a while. Then she said, "I believe you. I'm sorry he did that to you. But he's your father. He's the breadwinner. Just be nice to him, and I'll make sure you're not alone with him anymore."

I left home as soon as I could. I married this jerk, just to get out of the house. I didn't know how to work or do anything like that. I couldn't leave on my own.

On the outside, it looks like everything's fine with me. I have kids. I'm still married. I look okay.

But nothing changed inside me. I still can't stand to be touched. I hold my breath and stare at the ceiling every time we have sex. I can barely hug my own kids. The only good thing I've done for my kids is keep them away from my father. I say and do all the right things. But I don't feel like I'm alive anymore.

I'm angry at my father for what he did. My mother thinks she's supportive of me, because she believes me. But she can't see that I'm angry at her, too—for not doing anything about the truth. Even today, she's glad I act like nothing happened.

As angry as I am at my father, I'm much angrier at my mother.

And pornography can make you angry— in two different ways

My husband is always looking at porn magazines and videos, plus the computer, of course. The worst part is, he wants these videos on, and the pictures around, when we have sex.

It makes me angry. Aren't I good enough? Why should I have to compete with all these knockout models? It may turn him on more, but it turns me off. It feels like a real put-down to me. Like a reminder that I'm really nothing special. The more turned on these models make him, the more I feel like just the handy local place he can plug himself in!

Lately, he complains that he can't get turned on without this stuff. He says it's my fault. He says if I lost weight and went to the gym, he wouldn't have this problem.

And I could lose a few pounds, all right. But there's something about this whole thing that makes me really mad.

* * * *

I know that men like these girlie magazines and videos and stuff, but my boyfriend is so far into this that it makes me furious. What he likes seems really sick to me—scenes that look like the woman is ready for her gynecologist to give her an exam, and scenes that look disgusting instead of sexy.

There's even some that have kids in them! That's sick. But the worst is ones that show people getting cut and hurt. That's not about sex—it's about torture.

I get so sick to my stomach that it makes me angry. What does this say about my boyfriend? What kind of guy is he, anyway? Am I even safe with him? Are my kids? Does he really see us as a woman and kids—or as toys or future victims?

If he gets off on stuff that makes me sick and afraid, how can I trust him with us? That makes me furious!

Anger is natural and real. And there's a lot in the world that can make you angry. It's normal to feel angry.

But too many women lose themselves to anger. They let someone else's anger run their lives. Or they act out their own anger on others around them.

You're going to find out how to make sure it's you—not anger—that's in control of your life.

ASK YOURSELF...

1. Which of these stories remind you of times you've felt angry? (The details are different, but what feelings are the same?)

2. What types of things make you angry?

3. What are some of the ways you deal with your anger?

4. How do you react to others' anger?

5. Have you ever had problems because of how you were or what you did when you were angry?

6. Have you ever had problems because of how you reacted when someone else was angry?

7. Did you ever hurt someone while you were angry and lost it?

8. Has someone hurt you while they were angry?

2

Take Charge of Your Own Anger

You can't change the world. You can't make all the things that bother you go away. You can't stop feeling angry sometimes. But you *can* do two things to take charge of your own anger:

- You can change how you *deal* with your anger.

- You can change how you *react* to other people's anger.

To do this, you have to ask yourself a serious question: are you willing to *separate* what you *feel* from what you *do* about that feeling?

The first place to start is to see the *difference* between:

What You *FEEL*
and
What You *DO*

Here's what this means:

- In most of the stories you just read, the women first *felt* angry and then, right away, they either *did* something (wrong) about it *or* they shut down and pretended they weren't angry. Either way, they immediately went from their *feelings* to *doing* something. There was no pause, no S-P-A-C-E between the feeling and the doing. The process looked like this:

FEELDO

- You saw, in the stories, that what they *did* was either something wrong, or nothing. They felt relieved *at the time*—but it hurt them

20

later. For example, the wife who takes Valium dulls her anger in the short run, but is damaging her mind and body in the long run. The mother who beat her two-year-old felt relief during her outburst, but either killed him or hurt him in physical, emotional, and mental ways. Even though *doing something* right away *feels* good, it ends up hurting you—and others—later.

■ The reason they *did* foolish things is that there was *no S-P-A-C-E* between what they *felt* and what they *did*. When there's *no S-P-A-C-E* between the two, there's no time for understanding what went wrong, for thinking of different ways to react, for choosing the best way to react, or for taking any steps that could lead to positive outcomes. *FEELDO* leaves you trapped in a corner.

■ If you put some S-P-A-C-E between what you *feel* and what you *do*, it will look like this:

FEEL   DO
or

FEEL   DO
or

FEEL   DO

■ You get the idea. If there's S-P-A-C-E between *feeling* and *doing*, you give yourself a chance to see how you really *feel,* think about the impact on *you*, see what choices you really have, think about where the other person is coming from, decide how much time the event "deserves" you being angry about it, think about how much anger the event is "worth" feeling, decide what kinds of outcomes would be best for *you*—and *THEN* decide what to *do*.

■ You will NOT be making the S-P-A-C-E for the sake of the person you're angry at. It's for *YOU!* If the women in the stories had done this, the woman at work could have decided whether or not she could learn something from her boss. The woman with anorexia could have thought about getting counseling. Things would have gone better for *all* the women in *all* the stories if they had given themselves some S-P-A-C-E between what they *felt* and what they *did*.

ASK YOURSELF...

1. Think about a time you *felt* angry AND *did* something about it that (you can see now) later turned out to be bad for you.

2. How much S-P-A-C-E was there between what you *felt* and what you *did*?

3. Looking back now, what are some *other* things you could have done that might have had a better outcome?

Here's the hardest part: while you feel angry, you have to catch yourself *early* enough to make the S-P-A-C-E between what you *feel* and what you *do*. This is why you have to decide whether you are *willing* to know the difference between the two. Little kids, for example, *can't* tell the difference between feeling and doing, and as soon as they *feel* something, whatever they *do* about it seems automatic and "right" to them. That's why infants cry as soon as they feel hungry, and why they scream if they have to stay hungry for too long. They're using FEELDO, with no S-P-A-C-E "between what they feel and what they do. That's okay for infants and little kids."

But women—who are *adults*—don't cry out or scream if they're hungry. They *feel* hungry, *then they take time to decide what to do about it,* and then they *do* something. Because they've taken time to think about it, what they *do* is usually practical and sensible.

The same is true for anger. Immature women are adults in the physical sense, but are children when it comes to their feelings. They act just like little kids when they're angry. They use FEELDO, because their feelings— not their own minds, not their own judgment, not their own experience, not their own intelligence, not their own maturity, and *not their own womanly knowledge*—are in control of what they *do*. Women who are controlled by their feelings are just big children. They act out their anger like kids. Or they let themselves be ruled by some bully's anger. A *real woman* is in charge of what she does *no matter what she feels.*

Here's how to make the S-P-A-C-E between what you *feel* and what you *do.* To get good at it, *practice these steps in your mind* long before you get angry. If you practice these steps at least once a day, when you're in a good mood, they'll be easier to do when you're angry and you need them.

How to Make S-P-A-C-E Between What You Feel and What You Do

- Pay attention to *yourself,* not the other person or situation that makes you angry.

- Pay very close attention to what you *feel—physically—*when you're angry. Anger isn't just in your mind. It's also in your body. Where do you *feel* the anger? In your face? Your throat? Your stomach? Your forehead? Your arms? Notice where, on your *body*, you feel it.

- Focus on your physical feelings. Let yourself *feel* what you feel. This will help focus on *yourself—*where your control is—instead of on the other person.

- Let your physical feelings help you accept the fact that you *are* angry, and that you have the *right* to be angry.

- Think of a question that helps you do something good for yourself. For example, you might ask yourself, "Is this action, or person, or situation *worth* getting worked up about?," or "Is it worth getting worked up *this much* about it?," or "What is it about this action, or person, or situation that *makes* me so angry?," or "Is this person trying to *control me* with their anger?" You may think of other questions to ask yourself. Don't *do* anything yet about your answer—just be aware of it, while you let yourself feel your anger.

- Ask yourself: "What is the most low-key, *neutral* thing I could do that would show this person I am *not* affected by him or her, that he does *not* matter enough to 'fight back' with, that she does *not* have the power to make me lose control of my actions or to rule me?" This is how you stay in charge—instead of "giving in" by hitting, or yelling, *or* giving in to whatever they want, you *do* something that shows *you're* in control of yourself.

For example, the angry mother could have given her two-year-old a time-out. Or a hug. The woman at work could have asked her boss for more information about her performance.

The point: after getting really in touch with the anger you *feel,* pick something low-key you can *do* that will take the power *out* of what made you angry.

By following all these steps, you make a S-P-A-C-E between the anger you *feel* and what you *do.* In this S-P-A-C-E, you find ways to *do* things that lower the degree of your anger—or the impact *their* anger has on you.

Be sure to practice these steps when you *don't* need them, so you'll be good at using them when you *do* need them.

When you can separate what you *feel* from what you *do*—and you can put a S-P-A-C-E between them—you're on top of the first part of taking charge of your own anger.

You'll already be starting to change how you *deal* with your anger, and how you *react* to others' anger. There are more steps to go, but you're well on your way.

. ASK YOURSELF...

1. Think of someone you know who does things that trigger your anger.

2. Think back to what you've done in the past, when you felt angry towards this person and did not put any S-P-A-C-E between feel and do.

3. What would you do now, if you were in the same situation BUT you put a S-P-A-C-E between feel and do?

3

Seven Ways Other People Use Their Anger to Control You

Once you can put a S-P-A-C-E between how you *feel* and what you *do*, you've done something *many women can't do.* They're too wrapped up in their feelings. When many women get angry, they either take it out on the person by yelling, hitting, or other actions, *or* they shut down, pout, and refuse to talk or do anything. When someone is angry *at them,* many women give in and do what the angry person wants.

In all these cases, the women don't even know what's happening. But this won't happen to you. *You're* taking charge of your *own* anger. And you're taking charge of yourself when someone else is angry *at* you. You're *deciding* what to do*, before* you do it.

The next step is to take control of your own actions and reactions in seven angry situations you've probably seen a lot. There are seven specific ways other people can trigger your anger *or* control you with theirs. Each of these ways has its own trap—its own way of getting you to *do* exactly what the other person wants. Women who just do FEELDO will fall right into this trap. But by putting a S-P-A-C-E between what you *feel* and what you *do*, you'll be able to plan *in advance* how to deal with each specific angry situation—and its trap.

1. Acted-Out Anger

Acted-Out Anger means the person is taking out their anger physically. They might be hitting, yelling, throwing things, stomping out of the room, or doing any number of things that are easy to see and hear. Their target may be a desk, chair, wall, window, TV set, computer, anything physical—including, sadly, another person or other living creature. An example is the woman who couldn't stop hitting her two-year-old.

Acted-Out Anger's trap is that when you see how angry this person is—especially if they are acting out their anger on *you*—you will fall right into their game and start acting out your own anger as well. Or, you may do the opposite—completely cave in and let them boss you around. They either get you all worked up *or* they get to control you. Either way, they get you to *lose control* of what you *do* and fall victim to what you *feel*. It looks like this:

Acted-Out Anger

You get angry too, you lose control, you act like them OR you let them control you with their anger.	They "win" because you lost control of your actions OR because you let them boss you around when they're angry.

If you follow this pattern, they're in control—because you're *not* in charge of what you do. *They* are. You did what *they* wanted you to do—which means they get their way with you. And the arrows show you that if you react the way *they* want, they'll keep using Acted-Out Anger on you.

Instead, you can avoid the Acted-Out Anger trap by:

- putting a S-P-A-C-E between what you *feel* and what you *do*

- *doing* things that are *very different* from what they want you to do. For example, instead of yelling back, you could smile, stay low-key and calm, and say, "Looks like you're getting kind of worked up. Want to settle down and talk?" Sometimes, the best thing might be to *get away* from them.

Your goal at this point is *NOT* to change them, solve everything, or control them. Instead, your goal is to *keep yourself out of the trap* of their anger style, and keep them from controlling you. It looks like this:

Acted-Out Anger

You're calm, detached,
and in control of what you do.

They feel frustrated,
look foolish compared
to you, and have no control
over you OR of themselves.

The most adult and womanly thing you can do in the face of Acted-Out Anger is stay calm and in control—of yourself. When you react *your* way—*not* theirs—they'll stop using Acted-Out Anger on you.

2. Irresponsible Anger

Irresponsible Anger means the person is mad when you hold them accountable for something. They usually don't deny that the problem happened. But they blame *you* for the part of the problem that really was *their* fault. For example: you loaned money to someone, and they didn't pay you back when they said they would. You ask for the money, telling them they're late paying you back—and they say it's *your* fault for not reminding them

The trap of Irresponsible Anger is that you'll *let them* blame *you* for something that was *their* fault. Even if you're to blame for *part* of the problem, you are *not* responsible for *their* part. It looks like this:

Irresponsible Anger

You agree that
you are at fault for
the whole problem–
even though they are
to blame for at least
part of it.

They get away
with not taking
responsibility for
their actions, and
you carry more
responsibility than
is fair to you.

If you react the way *they* want you to, they'll keep using Irresponsible Anger on you.

Instead, you can avoid the Irresponsible Anger trap by:

■ putting a S-P-A-C-E between what you *feel* and what you *do*

■   *doing* things that are *very different* from what they want you to do. For example, refuse to take the blame for their part of the problem. If you did something that was part of the problem, you can mention it—but stick to the fact that *they* are to blame for *their* part. It looks like this:

Irresponsible Anger

You refuse to take any of the blame for *their* part—even if you admit that you are at fault in another way.	They can't blame you for what they did wrong, and they have to accept the fact that *they* are responsible for their part of the problem.

The best way to deal with Irresponsible Anger is to stick to the facts and refuse to be blinded by their failure to take responsibility. The arrows show that when you react the way *you* want to, they'll quit using Irresponsible Anger on you.

3. Self-Centered Anger

Self-Centered Anger means the person is angry that they have to follow the same rules as everyone else. They're angry because they want you to treat them "special," the "exception" to the rule. An example is the woman who shoplifted.

Self-Centered Anger's trap is that you may find it easier to give in to them than to make them follow the rules like everyone else. If you do this, you're letting this person decide what you will do. It looks like this:

Self-Centered Anger

You give in and treat them as "special" or the "exception"– despite what you want to do, or your values.	They get their way, they get you to go against what you want to do (and maybe even against your values), and *they're* in charge of your actions.

If you follow this pattern, you give up control of your own actions and let the other person decide what you'll do. You also may be going against your own value system, which will make you feel even less in control of yourself. If you react the way _they_ want, they'll keep using Self-Centered Anger on you.

Instead, you can avoid the trap of Self-Centered Anger by:

- putting a S-P-A-C-E between how you _feel_ and what you decide to _do_.

- refusing to treat them any differently from how you treat everyone else.

For example, reminding them that there are no "exceptions" and that no one is more "special" than anyone else. It looks like this:

Self-Centered Anger

You refuse to make an exception for them—you make them follow the rules.	They have to accept the fact that they are just like everyone else when it come to the rules—and you are in charge of your own actions.

You're not trying to put them down or make them "less" than anyone else. You're just making them follow the same rules as everyone else. You're also staying in charge of your _own_ actions. By reacting _your_ way instead of theirs, you stop them from using Self-Centered Anger on you.

4. Two-Faced Anger

Two-Faced Anger means the person is nice to someone's face, but works against them behind their back. They don't come out and tell the person that they have a problem with him or her or with something the person did. They tell everyone else, or they do something sneaky, instead.

Two-Faced Anger's trap is that you listen or go along with the person's anger, may agree or disagree—but, just like them, _you don't tell the person_ that there's a problem. "Everyone" knows that the man or woman has a problem with this person—everyone except the person, that is. It looks like this:

Two-Faced Anger

You listen to how angry they are at the other person, and you get angry "with" them—and you don't tell the other person either.	They gain power over you, because they got you to take their side AND to keep their secret from the other person.

If you go along with this, you're giving up your right to have your *own* feelings, make your *own* decisions, and choose for *yourself* how to deal with the other person. You've let someone else *make* you take their side. And on top of that, you're *also* helping them keep everything secret—which you know makes things get worse—instead of bringing it out in the open, where it could get fixed. Because you reacted the way *they* wanted you to, they'll keep using Two-Faced Anger on you.

The way to avoid the Two-Faced Anger trap is by:

- putting a S-P-A-C-E between what you *feel* and what you *do*.

- *doing* things that are *very different* from what they want you to do. For example, you can refuse to go along with what the angry person says or does. You can listen or watch, but you can also refuse to get involved. You also can tell them that they might be better off just bringing up the issue to the person they're angry at, instead of acting it out all over the place. What you'll be doing looks like this:

Two-Faced Anger

You listen or not, but you respond in a mild way that does *not* take sides. You stay calm and refuse to take their anger on as your own.	They see that they *can't* get you to feel the way *they* want you to feel. *You're* deciding how you feel and act.

The way to keep control of your own life when a person uses Two-Faced Anger is to stick to your own feelings, your own issues, and your own actions. Stay out of *their* problems and *their* feelings. If you react the way *you* want to, they'll stop using Two-Faced Anger on you.

5. Rigid Anger

Rigid Anger means the other person uses their anger as a way to *control* you. They yell, withdraw, badger, harass, intimidate, and even threaten you to get their way. They use *power* over you. Often, they use *physical* power. But they also may use the power of *their* money, *their* car, and other things you depend on them for. Their power comes from your *fear* and your *dependence.* An example is the woman who stays with her man even though she's afraid of him.

The trap of Rigid Anger is that it's easier to give in than to argue with them. But once you give in, they'll keep using their Rigid Anger anytime you disagree with them. It looks like this:

Rigid Anger	
You do what *they* want you to do, instead of what *you* want to do.	They get *their* way—and you lose control of *your* choices and actions.

If you go along with this, you feel *threatened* into doing what *they* want. You let them *bully* you into obeying them. You give them power over your choices. And you put your choices—and yourself—into a "second-rate" place. You're letting them run your life. The more you give in to them, the more they'll use Rigid Anger on you.

You can avoid the Rigid Anger trap by:

- putting a S-P-A-C-E between what you *feel* and what you *do.*

- *doing* things that are *very different* from what they want you to do. For example, you can stick with what *you* want to do, instead of letting *them* make your choices for you. It looks like this:

Rigid Anger

You do what *you* want to do, no matter what *they* think you should do.	They learn that they can't boss you around.

When you make your own choices, instead of letting yourself get bullied into doing things *their* way, you stay in charge of yourself. You keep your own power. You feel better and have more self-respect. Ironically, they probably will have more respect for you also—but you're still doing this for *yourself.* When you react *your* way, they'll stop using Rigid Anger on you.

6. Drinking/Drugging Anger

Drinking/Drugging Anger means either the person is angry *because* of the alcohol or drugs they've been taking, or they were already angry and what they took has made their anger worse. An example is the woman who had so much trouble quitting her drugs and alcohol.

Drinking/Drugging Anger's trap is that you try to deal with the user as if they're reasonable. When they use alcohol or drugs, they *aren't* reasonable—at least, not a reasonable *adult.* They're more like *un*reasonable *kids*, having a temper tantrum and not wanting to listen. It looks like this:

Drinking/Drugging Anger

You try to talk sense with them.	They get more *un*reasonable and their anger increases.

If you fall into this trap, you'll waste a lot of your time trying to reason with them. You'll also risk getting them angrier. Angry people on alcohol or drugs are a waste of energy. If you keep trying to treat them the way they expect, they'll keep using Drinking/Drugging Anger on you.

The way to avoid the Drinking/Drugging Anger trap is by:

- putting a S-P-A-C-E between what you *feel* and what you *do*.

- *doing* things that are *very different* from what they expect you to do. For example, you can refuse to deal with them while they're in that state of mind. It looks like this:

Drinking/Drugging Anger

You avoid
talking to them, and
you get away.
IF you talk to them,
it's only when they're
sober/straight.

They find
someone else
to take their
anger (and
unreasonableness)
out on.

At the very least, you'll be less bothered by them, because they won't take their anger out on you. At the very best, you'll be able to talk to them when they are sober or straight. But by avoiding their Drinking/Drugging Anger, you save your time and energy for *yourself.* When you react *your* way, they'll stop using Drinking/Drugging Anger on you.

7. Delusional Anger

Delusional Anger means that what makes the person angry is *not real*. It's a delusion, or even a hallucination, in their minds. This is very different from the guy who questions his girlfriend or the one who keeps telling his wife how fat and ugly she is. In both these examples, the men know very well what's true. They use the questions or the insults as ways to *control* the women. But when someone *hallucinates*, they actually see and/or hear things that *no one else* sees or hears.

With a delusion or a hallucination, they *really believe* something that you and everyone else *knows* is not true. Sometimes these beliefs are not even physically possible. For example, they might believe that you are physically probing their brain with wires. To the person who sees or hears them, delusions and hallucinations are much more real than a hunch or a gut feeling. Delusions and hallucinations are *just as real to them* as the physical world you see is to you.

Because delusions and hallucinations look and sound so real to the person, it's impossible to convince them that what they think is not true.

In this way, they are very much like the person with Drinking/Drugging Anger. Alcohol or drugs *also* can cause delusions and hallucinations in an otherwise normal person.

But some people have delusions and hallucinations even without taking drugs or alcohol. In these cases, the delusions or hallucinations come from physical problems inside their brains. Drugs or alcohol can make the problems even worse.

You also should know that delusions and hallucinations come and go. The person may be very reasonable and "with it" (meaning, in touch with reality) much of the time, and very "out of it" (meaning, *out* of touch with reality) at other times.

The trap with Delusional Anger is that you *know* what they're angry at *didn't happen.* So you try to be reasonable with them, or you laugh it off. In either case, your reaction will only make them angrier. It looks like this:

Delusional Anger

You laugh them off, or you try to explain that what they think happened did *not* really happen.	They are even more convinced that you're out to get them—so they get angrier, less predictable, and more dangerous.

If you go along with this, you'll waste time *and* put yourself at risk. You're trying to get them to deny something that is as *real* to them as the things *you* see and hear are to you. If you keep trying, they'll keep using Delusional Anger on you.

Because of how *real* their delusions and hallucinations are to *them,* the way out of the Delusional Anger trap is by:

■ putting a S-P-A-C-E between what you *feel* and what you *do.*

■ *doing* things that are *very different* from what they expect you to do. For example, you can let them know that you respect what they believe. Then, you have to let them know you did not do what they think you did. It looks like this:

Delusional Anger

You tell them you understand that they're angry because they think you did a certain thing. Then, you explain that you didn't mean it the way they took it, or you didn't know what you were doing at that moment.	They accept that you didn't mean it the way they thought, OR they decide that *you* misunderstood. You are in less danger.

With Delusional Anger, you're not trying to get to the truth as much as you're trying to lower their anger in a situation where you can't win. The reason you can't win has *nothing* to do with you. It's all about *their* delusions and hallucinations—which, sooner or later, may go away and be followed by new ones. When you react *your* way, they'll stop using Strange Anger on you.

You've now seen seven angry situations that used to *make* you angry or *make* you react the way the other person wanted you to. Now you know how to choose *your own reactions* in all seven cases—no matter how much the other person tries to control you.

ASK YOURSELF...

1. Think of a time when you saw someone doing Acted-Out Anger. How adult, versus childish, do they seem to you now? How did you react to them then? What different ways could you react to them now?

2. Think of a time when you saw someone doing Irresponsible Anger. How adult, versus childish, do they seem to you now? How did you react to them then? What different ways could you react to them now?

3. Think of a time when you saw someone doing Self-Centered Anger. How adult, versus childish, do they seem to you now? How did you react to them then? What different ways could you react to them now?

4. Think of a time when you saw someone doing Two-Faced Anger. How adult, versus childish, do they seem to you now? How did you react to them then? What different ways could you react to them now?

5. Think of a time when you saw someone doing Rigid Anger. How adult, versus childish, do they seem to you now? How did you react to them then? What different ways could you react to them now?

6. Think of a time when you saw someone doing Drinking/Drugging Anger. How adult, versus childish, do they seem to you now? How did you react to them then? What different ways could you react to them now?

7. Think of a time when you saw someone doing Delusional Anger. How did you react to them then? What different ways could you react to them now?

4

Decide Whether to Talk Now— When You're Angry
Skill #1

Y ou know how to put S-P-A-C-E between what you *feel* and what you *do*. You also know how to stay in charge of *your own* reactions when other people are angry.

Now you'll see how to stay in charge of yourself when *you're* angry. There are seven skills to use. It will take *all seven* before you can really work things out with the other person. No single skill will take care of all of it right away. But each skill plays a part, and each skill is needed.

In this chapter, we'll cover Skill #1: Decide Whether to Talk Now.

The minute you feel angry, make the S-P-A-C-E between that feeling and what you do—and *ask yourself* two questions:

1. **Do you want to talk things over with the other person, *right now*?** You may not want to talk things over at all. You may want to *stay* angry at them forever. Or, even if you *do* want to talk things over with them, you may not be ready *right now.* Let's be honest—sometimes, feeling angry can *feel good* for a while, because you feel so justified being angry at them.

If you want to stay angry at them forever, simply do everything you can to avoid them.

If you want to talk things over, but *not right now,* not while you feel so justified—*wait.* Do *not* do anything except remove yourself *until the moment you can answer "yes" to this question.*

The rest of the skills won't work until your answer to Question #1 is "yes."

37

2. **Even if *you* want to talk things over with this person, do *they* want to talk things over with *you*?** Just because *you're* ready to work on the anger with them *doesn't* necessarily mean *they're* ready! So even when you're ready, you still have to wait until *their* answer is "yes." None of these seven skills will work unless *both* you and the other person can answer "yes" to questions #1 and #2.

Here's something to be careful of. People who get angry in any of the seven ways we talked about earlier may *seem* like they *don't* want to talk things over with you. And that may be true. But the skills described in this book can build on even the *smallest shred* of willingness the other person may have. It helps if you stay open to the chance that they *may* want to work it out with you. It also helps if you start out by *assuming* they want to but they just need your help in using these seven skills.

If you ask them—or you just start using the skills—and nothing works, it's time to give up. We'll talk more about that in Skill #7. For now, we'll assume that both you and they are ready, so you can see how to use all the skills.

When your answers to both questions are "yes," you're ready to use the next six skills to take charge of your own anger. You might not always use all six. And you might use them in a different order. But the first skill is always the same—deciding if *both* you and the person you're angry at *want* to solve it *now.*

ASK YOURSELF...

1. Think of someone you've been angry at in the last two weeks. Did you want to stay angry, at least for a while? Did you (after a while) want to work it out with them? Did they want to work it out with you?

2. For you personally, what is the hardest thing about wanting to work it out with someone you're angry at? How much does pride get in the way? Fear? Hurt? What do you think you might lose by talking it over with them?

3. Think of someone you know who "always has to be right." Would they want to talk things over with someone they were mad at? How much like an adult —and how much like a child—do they seem to you, when they're angry?

5

Talk to the Right Person—When You're Angry
Skill #2

nce you've decided, with Skill #1, that you both want to talk things over, the next thing to do is use Skill #2: Talk to the Right Person.

What to Do

This isn't as easy as it sounds. For some reason, most women tell all their friends how angry they are at someone *before* they tell the person they're angry at. It looks like this:

You tell your friends how angry you are at this person.	Your friends tell you to either get over it or get even.	The other person has no idea there's a problem, so they can't work it out with you.
	OR	**OR**
	Your friends tell the the other person that you're angry.	The other person gets angry at you and/or your friends —and things get worse.

40

In either case, there is no room for Skill #1—deciding that you (and they) are ready to fix it. Instead, either the person doesn't know anything about your anger, or the anger increases and the chances of working things out get slimmer. In either case, you've just lost control of the situation, both to your friends and to the person you're angry at! They will decide what to do about your anger—when you should be the one who decides.

To stay in charge of your own anger, the best thing you can do for yourself is *go directly to the person you're angry at,* and tell them yourself that you're angry. *How* you tell them is going to make all the difference, and we'll talk about that in a few minutes. But for now, the important thing to know is that as soon as you decide that you (and they) are willing to at least talk things over, the best thing you can do for yourself is go tell *them.* It looks like this:

You tell the person (in the way you'll see *how* to tell them) that you're angry and you want to talk about it with them.

They either are willing to talk it over, or want to think about it first and talk it over later, or want to stay angry at you, or couldn't care less. In any case, they *know* you're angry at them, and you've given them a *chance* to talk things over with you.

No matter which of these ways they react, *you've* done the best you can to let them know you're angry and to give them a chance to talk it over with you. You've kept it between them and you. You haven't dragged in your friends or co-workers or relatives, or anyone else who's not involved. And you've taken control of *your own* anger.

How to Do It

But talking to the person you're angry at is only part of Skill #2. You *also* have to be in charge of *how* you talk to them. Here's why: *how* you talk is just as important as *what* you say. It looks like this:

You say: **"I'm mad, and it's *your fault!*"**
                      OR "I'm mad at *you!*"

They react: **"Oh, no! It's *your* fault!"**
                      OR "Well, *I'm* mad at *you!*"

This won't go very far, because *how* you talked to them made them feel defensive, challenged, and pushed into a corner. *How* you talked to them made them feel as if you think "all" of them is "bad." And your way of talking has not left any room for discussion with them.

Also, by making it their "fault," or "them," you give up *your* power and you let *them* be in charge of your feelings.

Instead, you can say it a different way—a way that doesn't accuse them, doesn't push them into a corner, and doesn't put all the blame on them. For example:

You say: **"I'm angry at you *for what you told the boss* about me."**

OR

"I'm upset because you *still haven't paid me back* the money you owe me."

OR

"I'm mad because you were *flirting with my boy friend*."

In these three examples, you focus on *what they did* that made you angry—their *actions*, instead of "all" of them. And you're being *specific*, instead of having a "general" anger towards them.

Remember that you are not going to fix everything with this skill (or any of the seven skills) *by itself*. But what you *will do* is talk about your anger in a way that will make them more willing to listen. And in a way that will make them more likely to talk it over with you.

The person may deny that they said anything bad to the boss, or come up with excuses about not paying you back, or swear they didn't mean anything about what they said to your boyfriend. *At this point,* neither of you is ready to resolve anything. All you're trying to do, at Skill #2, is go to the person you're angry at, bring up the subject, and start talking it over.

You've started with Skill #1: Decide Whether to Talk Now. You've gotten to Skill #2: Talk to the Right Person (in the right way). The rest of the skills, combined, will help you fix the problem between you and them.

ASK YOURSELF...

1. How often do you tell your friends before you tell the person you're angry at? What usually happens when you tell your friends first?

2. Who's the easiest person for you to tell you're angry at them? Who's the hardest person for you to say it to?

3. What's the hardest thing about telling someone you're angry at them? The easiest?

4. What are some bad results that came from how you said you were angry? What are examples of good results that came from how you said it?

6

Pay Attention to Their Feelings—
When You're Angry
Skill #3

Y ou've used Skill #1: Decide Whether to Talk Now. You've done
Skill #2: Talk to the Right Person. Now you're ready for Skill #3:
Pay Attention to *Their* Feelings. This is a crucial step towards staying in charge of your own feelings, and towards working things out with the
other person.

Let's start with what happens if you *don't* pay attention to their feelings. This is typical:

You're angry at someone.

You tell them you're *angry*, why it's *their* fault, how *right* you are about it, and how *they're* to blame not only for *this* problem, but for other problems also.	They get defensive, refuse to listen, say "Oh, yeah?" and start to prove how it's all *your* fault. And they get really angry at you.

The result is that *both* of you end up angry, nothing gets settled, and
the two of you don't get along anymore. Is this familiar to you?

But if you pay attention to *their* feelings *also*, there's a good chance
that two very different things will happen. First, they will feel as if they, as
a person, *matter*. They *count*. You're *not* treating them shabbily or like an
object that's in the way. Feeling like they *matter* as a person will make
them less defensive, less threatened, and less likely to shut you out. They'll
be more likely to listen.

44

Second, if you pay attention to their feelings, their anger will go *down*. Not low enough to "solve" everything right then. But low enough for them to *talk* with you about *your* anger. And that's your goal—getting them to talk it over with you. It looks like this:

You're angry at someone.

You tell them you're angry, *and that you can see* THEY'RE angry, annoyed, upset, or *whatever* you think they feel at the time. Then, you tell them you want to talk things over with them.	They feel like they count. *They're less defensive and more* willing to hear about your anger. They're more willing to talk things over with you.

In Skill #1, you decided you both were willing to talk. In Skill #2, you went to the person you're angry at. In Skill #3, you pay attention to *their* feelings, as well as your own. Once you pay attention to their feelings, and they're more willing to listen and talk, *how* you talk with them will be important again.

More About *What* You Say and *How* You Say It

Try this exercise: Frown, scowl, and look as *negative* and *critical* as you can. Then, say, "I'm so *happy!*"

Try another exercise: Smile, lift your eyebrows, and raise your eyes up. Then, say, "I'm so *down!*"

Now, stand up, cross your arms in front of you, tap one foot quickly on the floor, make the corners of your mouth point down, and frown. Then, say, "I'm a very patient woman. You can come talk to me any-time."

Hard to do? Does it feel strange? Out of sync? Torn in different directions? In all three cases, *what* you say doesn't match *how* you say it. It feels strange because you're giving *two very different messages* at the same time. In the first exercise, your face says you're negative and sour, but your words say you're happy. In the second exercise, your face says you're happy but your words say you're sad. In the third one, you body says you're closed, impatient, and unapproachable, but your words say you're patient and open.

So far, there are two things to get from these exercises:

1. **People will believe you *only* when *what* you say matches *how* you say it.** When your *what* and *how* contradict each other, people feel nervous around you.

2. **If your *what* and *how* don't match, people will believe your *how* and not your *what*.** In the first exercise, they'll believe you're critical and negative because of *how* you say it, and they *won't* believe you're "happy" even though that's *what* you say. In the second exercise, they'll believe you're *happy* because that's *how* you say it, and they won't believe *what* you say. In the third exercise, they'll believe you're impatient and closed, because of *how* you say it—regardless of *what* you say.

These two points show you that *how* you talk is just as important as *what* you say.

When you're angry, paying attention to *both*—*what* and *how*—keeps you in charge of your anger. First, let's look again at the typical way it goes when you don't pay attention to the other person's feelings:

You're angry at someone.

You tell them you're *angry*, why it's *their* fault, how *right* you are about it, and how *they're* to blame not only for *this* problem, but other problems *also*.	They get defensive, refuse to listen, say "Oh, yeah?" and start to prove how it's all *your* fault. And they get really angry at *you*.

Your *what* is negative and critical—telling them it's their fault, that you're right, and how they're to blame for lots of problems. The odds are that *how* you say it—your face, body language, and tone of voice—also are negative and critical. Because both your *what* and *how* are the same, the person *believes* that you *mean* what you're saying—that you're right, they're wrong, and it's all their fault. No wonder they get defensive!

And, going a step further: when *how* you come across about your feelings is so strong, it sounds to the other person as if *only you* are going to get what you want from this conversation. When your *how* is so strong about only you, there's no room for them or their feelings. Why *should* they try to work things out with you?

It's a different story when you let them know that they count also. Let's look again at what happens when you pay attention to *their* feelings:

You're angry at someone.

You tell them you're angry, *and that you can see* THEY'RE angry, annoyed, upset, or *whatever* you think they feel at the time. Then you tell them you want to talk things over with them.	They feel like they count. *They're less defensive and more* willing to hear about your anger. They're more willing to talk things over with you.

This time, your *what* includes you *and* them. You're angry *and* you know that they have feelings as well. It's not just about you. And the odds are that your *how* matches what you say—straightforward, open, willing to listen as well as talk. Because your *how* matches your *what,* they believe you mean what you say—that you're angry, you know *they* have their own feelings also, and that you want to talk *with* (not against) them.

This time, your *how* has room for both of you. You want to talk things over for *both* of your sakes. That's why they're more likely to be willing to talk and work things out with you.

And back to *you.* By paying attention to both your *what* and your *how,* you keep *yourself* in charge of your anger. You don't let your anger go off by itself, and you don't let the other person shut you and your anger out.

At Skill #1, you decided you and they were willing to try to work things out. At Skill #2, you went to the person you're angry at. And at Skill #3, you keep things going by paying attention to *their* feelings, as well as your own.

And *you*—not your anger—are staying in charge of your actions.

ASK YOURSELF...

1. Which of these feelings do women let themselves feel: angry, loving, jealous, happy, brave, afraid?

2. What feelings come most easily to you?

3. What feelings are hard for you to admit you feel? What's hard about it?

4. Who's the easiest person for you to talk to, about your feelings?

5. What happens to women who can't, or don't, talk to anyone about their feelings?

Checklist

1. Look over the list below.

2. For each item, notice *all* the feelings you might have at the same time.

3. Notice *which feelings* are okay for you, and *which feelings* make you feel uncomfortable.

- ❏ Love
- ❏ Babies
- ❏ Bars
- ❏ Home
- ❏ Police
- ❏ Family
- ❏ Blood
- ❏ Men
- ❏ Husband
- ❏ Fear
- ❏ Significant other
- ❏ Child abusers
- ❏ Divorce
- ❏ Counseling
- ❏ Prisons
- ❏ Drugs
- ❏ Church
- ❏ Your face
- ❏ Boyfriend
- ❏ Your body
- ❏ Your child/children
- ❏ Marriage
- ❏ Your work
- ❏ Money
- ❏ Independence

7

Find Something in Common—
When You're Angry
Skill #4

You've done Skill #1, deciding you're both willing to work things out. You've done Skill #2, going to the person you're angry at. You did Skill #3, paying attention to the other person's feelings. And now you're ready for Skill #4: Find Something in Common with the person you're angry at.

You are not ready to find something in common until you've done the first three skills. This is because without the first three, you and the other person would have either gotten into a bad argument, ignored each other, or dropped it after an uneasy start. The first three skills have gotten you to a place where you and they can start to talk things over.

But—Skill #4 isn't going to "solve everything" yet either. Skill #4: Find Something in Common is going to help you and the other person work together better on it. You're still building towards working things out. And *you're* staying in charge of your actions, instead of letting your anger take over.

Finding something in common is important because it lets each of you get something for yourself out of talking and working things out. When there's something in it for both of you, you're both more likely to keep working on it.

You can think in advance about what you have in common with people you sometimes get angry at. The relationship might be what you have in common—your marriage, your friendship, the fact that you work in the same building with each other every day. Activities might be what you have in common—taking your kids to the same daycare, or working out. What you and a co-worker might have in common is the need to look good to your boss. The point is to find something in common that makes *both* of you willing to keep working on the thing that makes you angry.

50

Let's look again at the conversation when you pay attention to the other person's feelings, and then you'll see how to move to finding something in common.

You're angry at someone.

You tell them you're angry, *and that you can see* THEY'RE angry, annoyed, upset, or *whatever* you think they feel at the time. Then you tell them you want to talk things over with them.	They feel like they *count. They're less defensive and more willing* to hear about your anger. They're more willing to talk things over with you.

Now that you've paid attention to their feelings, and they're willing to hear your side and talk things over with you, the next thing you can do is tell them what you both have in common. Your part of the conversation could go something like these examples:

You pay attention to their feelings:

"I'm angry about something you did. I can see that you're pretty upset yourself right now. Let's talk it over."

After they agree—you find something in common:

"Good. We're friends. We've got to work this out."

OR

"Good. We both want to the boss to see that we're getting along."

Or whatever else fits the situation. What you find in common helps *both* of you keep working at it.

Skill #1 got you to decide that both of you were willing to talk. Skill #2 got you talking to the person you're angry at. Skill #3 got you to pay attention to their feelings, as well as yours. Skill #4 helps you find something in common, so you're both motivated.

And your anger *isn't* controlling your actions. *You* are.

ASK YOURSELF...

1. Who are three people you often get angry at?

2. What do you have in common with each of them?

8

Depersonalize the Situation—
When You're Angry
Skill #5

Y ou've used four skills so far: deciding that both you and the other person are willing to talk, going to the person you're angry at, paying attention to their feelings (as well as yours), and finding something in common. Now you're ready for Skill #5: Depersonalize—which means *don't* take things personally.

It's easy to take things personally, especially when you're angry. But when you take things personally, three things work *against* you:

- **You feel as if *you*, the whole person, are being judged as "bad."** The truth is, what's being judged is *something you did— not* all of who you are.

- **You get defensive, so you can't listen.** As you know, working things out with the other person means you'll have to listen to what they say. If you take things personally, your defensiveness will stop you from listening.

- **You can't work things out with the other person.** To talk about your anger and their feelings, you have to be able to talk! When you take things personally, you've lost control of your ability to talk calmly enough to resolve anything.

If you take things *personally*, you're letting yourself act like a *child*—not an adult. You're not putting any S-P-A-C-E between what you *feel* and what you *do*. That S-P-A-C-E—and the *thinking* you do in that S-P-A-C-E— make all the difference.

How to *Not* Take Things Personally

1. **Remind yourself that it's not about *all* of you.** If someone's mad at you, they're mad about something you *said* or *did*. They're not angry at the whole person you are. They're not angry at your life, your birth, your history, your smarts, your strengths, and the billions of other things that make you who you are. Remind yourself that their anger is *limited* to *specific things,* not "all of" *you.*

2. **Ask yourself, "How much is their anger about what *I* did or said, and how much of their anger is about *them*?"** What you did or said may have hurt them in some ways. You have to be honest with yourself and accept that they may have a right to be angry. You still may think you did or said the right thing, or that they deserved it—but here you have to look at it from *their* point of view.

   Then you have to ask yourself how much of their anger is about *them.* Some people go through life angry a lot of the time, and they look for other people to take it out on. Ask yourself how much the person's anger is justified, or at least understandable, and how much of it really is about *them.*

3. **Ask yourself if what you *think* is going on really *is* going on.** You may have heard *rumors* about them being angry at you. You may have heard *part* of what they said, and filled in the rest— *incorrectly*—in your own mind. You may be *wrong* about thinking they're mad at you. Or, if they *are* angry, you may have the wrong idea about *why,* or *how much.* Before jumping to conclusions and making assumptions, get out of *your personal* mindset and find out where *they're* really at.

   And, before we get into how to talk to the other person in a depersonalized way, there is one more key item:

4. ***Do not MAKE* it personal!** It works against you if you *take* things personally, and it also works against you if you *make* it personal about *them.* Use the steps in the next section, to talk to them in a *depersonalized* way.

How to Talk in a Depersonalized Way

You've used the first four skills already: decided you both were willing to talk, went to the person you're angry at, paid attention to their feelings (as well as your own), and found something in common. Now you're ready to talk to them *about your anger* in a *depersonalized* way.

Here are the steps to follow:

1. ***Own* your anger.** Do *not* say, "*You made* me angry!"—because that gives *them* power over you. You're saying that *they* control *your* anger.

   Instead, say, "*I'm* angry at you!"—because that keeps *you* in charge of your anger. To be in charge of your own anger, *you* have to *own* it.

2. **Talk about their *actions* or *words, NOT* about *them.*** Do *NOT* say,

   "*You're* a jerk!" or "*You* don't know what you're doing!" It's not *them,* the whole person, you're angry at.

   You're angry at something they *did* or *said.* So, instead, tell them, "I'm angry at you *calling me stupid!*" or "I'm angry at you for *hitting on my boyfriend!*" or "I'm angry at you for *telling the boss I lied.*"

   When you talk about being angry at what they *did* or *said,* that's a lot *less* personal than saying you're angry at *them.* It also gives you room to talk about *why* they did or said it, what *you* could do or say differently to them, how *they* could act or talk differently to you or about you. It gives both of you room to change things for the better—by learning about yourselves and each other.

3. **Find out what's *behind* their actions or words.** Do *NOT* assume anything! It will make you sound like you're *accusing* them, and things will get worse instead of better. For example: do *not* say, "I'm angry at you calling me stupid. *Are you trying to make me look bad?*"

   Instead, *ask* why they did what they did or said what they said. And be careful *HOW* you ask. Make sure it doesn't sound like an accusation, like "Are you trying to make me look bad?" sounds.

Say: "I'm angry at you calling me stupid. *Why did you say that?*" Or, "I'm angry at you for hitting on my boyfriend. What's going on?" Or, "I'm angry at you telling the boss I lied. What did you do that for?"

By *asking*—instead of assuming or accusing—you are more likely to learn something.

After you've asked why they acted or spoke the way they did, a lot depends on the reasons they give you. Maybe they were getting even with you for something *you* did or said. Maybe they were joking—or thought they were, or want *you* to think they were. Maybe they had no idea what they were saying or doing at the time. And maybe you misinterpreted them—or maybe what you thought (or heard) happened *didn't* happen. A lot depends on what you find out here.

If they were getting even with you for something, you can make a deal with them—you'll stop (or change) if they do. If they were joking, you need to tell them (in a way described below) that you would like them to stop making those kinds of jokes. If they were not aware of what they were doing or saying, you can ask them (in a way described below) to be more careful when they talk about you. If you misinterpreted them—or if the event didn't even happen—you can apologize (in a way described below) and thank them for talking about it with you.

4. **Talk about *specific changes* you want.** Do *NOT* be vague, general, or personal. If you want them to change their behavior or words, *don't* say they should "show more respect" or "be careful of" what they say. These ways of talking are too general and too easy to interpret in different ways. What *they* call "respect" or "being careful of" what they say may be very different from what *you* want.

Instead of being too general, get *very* specific. For example:

"I'm angry at you calling me stupid. Why did you say that?" If they say they were joking, a specific, depersonalized way to ask for the change you want is: "Please don't make jokes like that about me anymore."

This is much more specific than "Be careful of what you say." It's also much less accusatory and much less personal. You can't control whether they change their behavior or not. But you've given them a chance by speaking up, and you can decide whether or how to deal with them, depending on what they do.

If you say, "I'm angry at you for hitting on my boyfriend. What's going on?," their answer might be that they "must have been drunk."

Whether you believe them or not, a specific and depersonalized way to ask for the change you want is to say something like, "Please pay more attention to what you're doing." You can't control their actions, but you've let them know what you want. You can decide later whether or how to relate to them, depending on what they do.

If you tell them, "I'm angry at you telling the boss I lied. What did you do that for?," they may say, "Well, you *did* lie. You called in sick, but you really weren't." You can ask for the change you want by saying something like, "I'd like you to keep what you know about my personal life separate from work." Again, you can't control their actions. But you can make them aware of what you want. You also can decide how close a friend you want to be, depending on what they do after you've asked for a change.

Depersonalizing makes it possible for you and the other person to talk about the things that make you angry—and about changes that can help.

You've used Skill #1, deciding that both of you are willing to talk. With Skill #2, you went directly to the person you're angry at. In Skill #3, you paid attention to their feelings (as well as your own). In Skill #4, you found something in common between the two of you. And in Skill #5, you've started talking about your anger in depersonalized ways.

ASK YOURSELF...

1. What are examples of people you know "pushing your buttons"—making personal comments that they know will "get you" angry?

2. How do you usually react when they do this?

3. How does your usual reaction make you feel?

4. What could you say that would depersonalize these situations?

9

Get to the Real Issue(s)—When You're Angry
Skill #6

The first five skills got you—and the other person—ready to get to the *real issue*. You decided that both of you were willing to talk, you went to the person you're angry at, you paid attention to their feelings (as well as your own), you found something in common, and you depersonalized the anger. All these skills have to be done before you (or they) can use Skill #6: Get to the *Real* Issue(s) about your anger (and theirs).

First, let's take a look at what the **real** issue means.

The *Real* Issue

When you're angry, it happens on two different levels. The first level is all the *details* that you're angry about. For example: someone cut you off on the freeway, someone didn't call you when they said they would, you didn't get the raise you deserve, your husband lied to you, you can't afford the car you want, your kids disobeyed you, or your boyfriend hit you. All these facts are the *details* that you're angry about.

But it goes deeper than that. The second level is what the details *mean* to you, what the details *say about* you, and what the other person *thinks* of you. The second level is what the details *mean* to you—*about* you.

Here are examples of how the first level—the *details*—relates to the second level—what the details *mean* to you, *about* you:

Details	Possible meaning *to you–about you*
Someone cuts you off on the freeway.	You're *nobody.*
	They think you're nobody.
	You *don't matter.*

Someone didn't call you when they said they would.	You're *second-class.* You're *not important.* You *don't matter.*
You didn't get the raise you deserve.	You're not good enough. You're stupid. You don't really deserve the raise. *Your boss* thinks you're nobody. You *don't matter.*
Your husband lied to you.	You're *not important.* You're *not sexy.* You're *not lovable.* You *don't matter.*
You can't afford the car you want.	You're worthless—just like your old car. You're *less* than others. You *don't matter.*
Your kids disobeyed you.	You get *no respect.* You're a *bad mother.* You *don't matter.*
Your boyfriend hit you.	It's *your* fault. You're *not lovable.* You're not good enough. **You're worthless.** You *don't matter.*

The first level—the *details*—catch your attention. But the second level—what the details *mean* to you, *about you*—is where your anger comes from.

Another way to look at the two levels:

Details = Symptoms (like a sore throat or a cough)
What the Details *Mean* to You, *About You* = Real Issue (like
                                        strep throat or a cold)

A sore throat or cough tells you something's wrong, but they are only the *symptoms.* You can't really cure or "fix" them until you know the *real issue*—is it strep throat or only a cold?

In the same way, the *details*—the guy cutting you off on the freeway, not getting the raise—are the *symptoms* that you notice. But the *meaning about you*—that you're worthless, that you don't matter—is the *real issue* that triggers your anger.

To get to the heart of your anger, and to resolve it, you have to talk about the *real issue,* not the symptoms.

How to Talk About the Real Issue

If you talk only about the *symptoms,* you'll never get to the *real issue.* Instead, you and the other person will go round and round over the details (symptoms), and things will get worse. Here's an example:

You:	"When will you pay me back the money you borrowed?
Other Person:	"Oh, do you need it right now?"
You:	"What do you mean, 'do I need it right now'? Last time you borrowed money from me, it was a year before you paid it back. This time, you said you'd pay in two weeks. It's been a month and a half."
Other Person:	"It wasn't a year, it was eight months. I said I'd pay you back as soon as I got my overtime check. It should have been here by now, but I still don't have it."
You:	"Well, if you'd follow up at work, maybe you'd get your check sooner. You just let things slide, and that's why things are never on time."
Other Person:	"Look who's talking! Remember the money I loaned you to fix your old car, and it wasn't till you sold the damn thing that you paid me back!"
You:	"The only reason that car had to be fixed is that I loaned it to *you,* and you *wrecked* it! You should have paid for the repairs in the first place!"
Other Person:	"Oh, yeah? Well......"

Is this familiar? Do you see how many other issues get into the conversation? How close are you to getting your money back? This conversation will keep getting worse, as more and more *details—symptoms—* are brought into it. In this type of conversation, you might lose your money *and* your friend.

To get to the *real issue,* you have to get past the symptoms.

You:	"When will you pay me back the money you borrowed?"
Other Person:	"Oh, do you need it right now?"
You:	"The big deal isn't the money. I feel taken advantage of when you're slow to pay it back."
Other Person:	"You mean, like I'm stealing it?"
You:	"No. It's like I don't count as a person. When you take your time paying it back, it feels like you don't think I'm important."

You can't control their reaction. But you've left out all the details (symptoms), and you've told them what their slow repayment *means* to you (the real issue). They may say, "Oh, I see. No problem. I'll pay you back tomorrow." They may say, "I never thought of it that way." They may be silent because no one's ever gotten to the real issue before.

You can't control their reaction. But by getting to the real issue, you give both of you a chance to talk things over. And sometimes, by getting to *your* real issue, you help the other person get to *theirs.*

When you get to the other person's real issue also, it's easier for *both* of you to talk about what bothers you and what you want from each other. One of the things you may find out is that sometimes *your real issue—* what their words or actions *meant to you* about *you—is not* what the person meant to say about you. They may even be surprised to hear how you took what they said. How you took it, and how that felt to you, are *real.* But the source may have been their *blindness,* not their ill will. Your friend may not have realized that returning the money late made you feel unimportant. Getting to the real issue helps you find this out. It helps resolve your anger.

However, there *are* times when the other person *meant* it in the way you took it. In these cases, your *real issue* changes.

Sometimes the Real Issue Changes

In the examples so far, you and the other person are able to resolve things because of Skill #1: You *both* want to work on the issues. But there also are times when the other person does *not* want to work things out with you. They may purposely *want* to put you down, and it's not a misunderstanding at all. In these cases, you have *two* real issues:

(1) The meaning *to* you, *about* you, of their words or actions.

(2) The fact that they do *not* want to work things out with you and, instead, they said what they said, or did what they did, because they *want* you to feel bad.

If you get even with them, yell in their face, call them names back, hit them, or react in *any* way that shows you're angry, guess who wins? They *got* you. Their nasty words or actions *got* to you. They have *power* over you.

Or, if you give in and just *take* it from them, you *still* give them power over you. You cave in, give up, and feel bad about yourself—which is exactly what they *want.* When you strike back *and* when you give up, you're letting them control you with their anger.

The hard part is that both types of reactions—striking back or giving up—are natural. This is because of your *first* real issue: the *meaning* of their words or actions is that you are *nothing* and you *don't matter.* So, of course you feel angry. It's hard enough to put a S-P-A-C-E between what you *feel* and what you *do,* when you're angry.

But even harder, your *second* real issue makes it worse—you realize they *want* you to feel bad, and that makes you even angrier. Their doing it *on purpose* gives your anger a double-whammy.

Many women have trouble staying in control of their reactions to the second real issue, even if they can stay in charge of themselves on the first real issue. This means that even if many women *could* stay in charge of their own anger when they feel put down, they often *can't* stay in charge when they know the put-down was *on purpose.* They feel trapped in a corner. Either they start fighting their way out—or they cave in, blame themselves, and feel worse about themselves. *Either way,* they let their own anger, and someone else's anger, control them.

Here's how to get out of this trap:

1. ***Do NOT try to talk or reason with this person.*** When you *know* that their goal is to make you feel bad, Skill #1 cannot take place. So none of the other skills will work with this person.

2. *Let yourself feel the anger you feel.* It's real, you know the source, and it's okay to *feel* it.

3. *Make a* S-P-A-C-E *between your anger and your actions.* In this S-P-A-C-E, tell yourself that your *first* real issue—feeling bad because of what this person is saying or doing—has to give way right now to your *second* real issue—the fact that they're doing it on purpose, and you want to stay *in charge* of your own actions.

   When you give yourself the S-P-A-C-E to focus on the second real issue, you want to decide what you can do or say that will take away the other person's power over you. Remember that they want to be able to *get* to you. So what can *you* do or say that looks like they *didn't* make you feel bad?

   One way might be to ignore them. Another might be to smile and nod your head in a friendly way. Another might be to touch their arm and say, "I'm glad you can be honest about how you feel." There is no "magic" way that will always work. *You* have to decide what you can do or say that will make you look *unaffected* by their words or actions. *Un-"got"* by them.

4. **Get away from them.** When their goal is to put you down and "get" you, hanging around with them will only make things worse for you. You're *not* going to be able to resolve any real issues with someone whose goal is to "get" you.

When you have to take all these steps for the second real issue, you still will have your angry feelings to deal with—*later,* when you're away from them, and they won't know. In the next chapter, we talk about how to deal with your anger *later.*

One more thing: sometimes, when you're dealing with a person who does *not* want to work things out with you, and you have to deal with this fact as the second real issue, you may have to get some *authority* behind you. For example: If you're being attacked (by threats or by getting hit) you need to get the police. If you're being called names at work, you have to talk to your boss or your Human Resources person about harassment. If you're being harassed by another inmate, you may have to get help from the warden—or from the prisoners who are running things.

After You've Discussed the Real Issue—
If They're Working With You
(and are not trying to "get" you)

In situations where the other person *does* want to work things out with you, there is one more step to take after you've talked about the real issue: you and the other person have to decide what each of you will *do,* based on your discussion. For example, they may agree to pay you back more quickly from now on: you may agree to be more specific about when you need the money back.

Once you decide what each of you will do, you then have to *do* it. If you don't, there's likely to be another round of anger later on.

In all these situations and examples, you've done Skill #6, Get to the Real Issue(s). This is where issues get solved and anger gets resolved.

ASK YOURSELF...

1. What are three things people do or say that make you angry? (These are the details, or the symptoms.)

2. For each one: what meanings about you (the real issues) do you get from these examples?

3. In what ways might you be uncomfortable talking about the real issues with someone you're angry at?

4. In what ways might you be comfortable talking about the real issues with someone you're angry at?

10

Drop the Grudge—When You're Angry
Skill #7

You've done Skill #1, deciding both of you were willing to talk. You did Skill #2 and went to the person you're angry at. You used Skill #3, paying attention to the other person's feelings (as well as your own). You did Skill #4 and found something in common. In Skill #5, you depersonalized how you talked about it. And you did Skill #6, getting to the real issues (and you did what you agreed to do). It sounds like you're done with your anger skills—but we still have Skill #7: Drop the Grudge. This is harder—and more important—than you think.

There are *three parts* to dropping the grudge. The first part comes *right after* you and the other person got to the real issues and agreed about what each of you would do—but *before* you come through with what you said you'd do.

Here's why: if you *don't* drop the grudge against this person, you *won't* do what you agreed to do. Or, you'll do it in a half-hearted or *grudging* way. And the anger between the two of you will come back—worse than before. To stay in charge of your anger, you have to *let go* of grudges.

Letting go is hard—especially of grudges. Once again, you have to face the fact that *either* you *or* anger (yours, or the other person's) is going to be in charge. Holding onto the grudge might feel justified. It probably feels *good*. But it gives all your power to your *anger*, instead of to your*self*. Here's how to let go of your grudge in order to do what you agreed to do:

How to Drop the Grudge So You Can Act Now

1. **Remember to *depersonalize*.** What they did wasn't about you—it was about *them*.

67

2. **You've already had your say.** They already know how you felt, and you know how they felt. You don't have to hash over the same stuff again.

3. **You have something to gain.** You're *not* "giving in" or "giving up" when you do what you said you'd do. You're doing your part of fixing the problem and working things out with them.

4. **You have nothing to lose.** You're doing the right thing by doing your part. If they don't do their part, you didn't "lose" anything or become a "fool." *They* did—because they lost control of their anger and let it boss them around.

If you keep these things in mind, it's easier for you to do the *first part* of dropping the grudge—and to do what you agreed to do. When you do your part, you help fix the anger between you and the other person. And you stay in charge of *your* anger.

The *second part* of dropping the grudge is more long-term. It can apply to one person, but it also applies to the general ways you deal with your anger and hold grudges.

Holding grudges can give you something to *hold onto*. It can make you feel very self-righteous. But the bad part is, it keeps you *angry*. You're *not* "wrong" to feel this way. But it works against you. The longer you hold on to grudges and anger, the more *they* take control of *you*. That's why you have to let go of them—so *you* can be in charge.

Letting Go of Grudges in General

Letting go is hard. Let's look at the steps and see what's hard about each step.

Step 1: Denial. Denial means you *can't see* how the grudges you hold are controlling you. Even if you "know" in your mind that they control you, it's hard to *believe* it in your guts. Why? Because it's hard to admit you're letting something *control* you.

Step 2: Giving them up. Like alcohol, drugs, gambling, smoking, workaholism, or a lot of other things that aren't good for you, grudges are hard to give up. They make you feel righteous, justified, like a winner. They make you feel on top of things.

But they have their "morning after," too. They take over your thoughts. They make you focus on the negative. They take a lot of your time. They cost you your health and your money. They take away your energy. They can make you lose your job, your friends, your family. They block out the good things—including people—in your life.

And like other addictions, *they take charge of your life.* Like all addictions, your grudges, and the people you have grudges against, *control you.*

Giving up your grudges leaves a big hole in your life—*for a while.* That's why most addicts can't quit for long. It takes an *adult* to give up what's destroying her.

Step 3: Healing. While you're giving up the grudges, the most *painful* part—the part that makes quitting so hard for addicts—is the fact that *healing hurts.*

Think of a time you cut your hand. The instant the cut happens, you don't feel anything—you're in shock, you're numb, you don't feel any pain. But as soon as the cut starts to *heal,* it really hurts.

It's the same for healing *emotionally,* in your *guts.* The hole in your life is what hurts when the grudge starts to leave. The loneliness, the feelings of being left out, not mattering, guilt, shame. Like any addiction, holding grudges fills the hole *for a while.* But they're only short-term fillings. It takes more and more of them to keep that hole filled. The only way to *really* fill that hole in your guts is something we'll talk about later, in Step 4. But grudges, like other addictions, *don't* keep that hole filled. So you keep getting more and more things to be angry about, more and more people to get angry at, to fill that hole. And when you quit the short-term filler, that hole opens up again—and you hurt.

You'll hurt in different ways. You'll try to *hide* all these hurts, because it's hard to admit you feel them. But you'll go through the same things as the heroin or coke addict having physical (and emotional) withdrawal. Here's what you'll feel *inside,* whether you'll admit it to anyone else or not:

- A *lot* of **anger**—even more anger than you thought you had. You'll want to *show* more anger, in worse ways. And you'll get angry *more easily* than you did before. You'll get angry over *small* things, not just big ones.

- *Fear.* You'll get afraid of things you didn't know you were afraid of. You'll fear small things that don't bother anyone else. You'll fear things that aren't happening. You'll feel afraid in a general way. You'll have trouble knowing what specific things are making you feel afraid.

■ *Sadness*. You'll feel sad about things from the past. Feeling happy will make you feel sad. You'll feel sad for no reasons at all. You'll feel sad at times when nothing around you is making you feel that way.

■ *Guilt*. You'll feel guilty because of what you did in the past. You'll feel guilty because of what you didn't do. You'll feel guilty when you have a good time. You'll feel guilty when you're sad.

■ *Depression*. This is different from sadness. *Sadness* means you feel down, you know it, and (if you can admit it to yourself) you feel like crying. But *depression* means you *don't feel anything*. You may be shocked to learn that anger was the *only* feeling you let yourself have. Your depression may make you feel like jumping into the hole you feel inside.

Healing *hurts* in these ways. That's why it's so hard to go through the healing step, and to give up the grudges in the first place. That's why *many women*, like most addicts, *can't quit*. It takes a *real woman*—that is, an adult—to give up the grudges and go through the healing process.

When all these feelings come up in you, the way to *heal* is:

■ Do *NOT* deny your feelings, ignore them, talk yourself out of them, or "do something" about them. *Just feel them*. Give yourself the time and space to feel them.

■ Let yourself *feel* everything that you feel. Different feelings will come and go *if you let them*. If you *don't* let them, they'll come anyway, but they'll stay *locked up inside you*—which is what caused all your anger and grudges in the first place. If you let them come, feel them, and let them go, you will heal. *You will get over them without denying them or letting them build up.*

It's tempting to hold onto the grudges in self-defense. But a *real woman* lets herself heal from her anger and grudges.

Step 4: Taking back control of your life. This is your payoff. After you get past your denial, give up your grudges, feel the hole inside, and let yourself heal, you're ready to fill that hole with positive things *you* choose, that are *good* for you. When you take back control of your *anger*, you're ready to take back control of your own *life. That's* womanly.

The *first part* of dropping your grudge is to be able to do what you agreed to do. The *second part* of letting go is dropping grudges in general—and healing.

The *third part* of dropping the grudge is when your *second* real issue is that the other person *doesn't* want to work things out with you. In Chapter 9, we talked about the person who *purposely* wants to put you down and make you feel bad. You saw how to avoid talking or reasoning with them, how to feel your own feelings, and how to make a S-P-A-C-E between what you feel and what you do. You saw how to show them that you're *un-got*—and to leave. Now you're ready to see how to deal with your anger *later,* when you're away from them.

How to Drop the Grudge When
the Other Person Wants to Get You

When the other person *doesn't* want to work things out with you, and wants to *get* you by putting you down, you have to show that they *didn't* get to you—and then leave. That's the end of having to put up with them.

But it's *not* the end of dealing with your anger. If you just blow it off, it will just build up. After a while, you'll be holding grudges—and losing more and more control of your anger *and* your life. So you *have to* deal with your anger after you get away from the person who's out to *get* you.

Step 1: Admit you're angry. Women often pretend they're not angry about these people. That's why they get stuck holding grudges—and letting anger control their lives.

Instead, admit *to yourself* that you're angry (and maybe even *hurt)* because of the other person trying to put you down. Remember that you have to know how you *feel* so you can take steps to deal with it.

Step 2: Depersonalize. What they said—and their need to put you down—tell you more about *them* than about *you.* You were the scapegoat for all their problems, but their problems are about *them—not you.* Even though they may say it's your fault, it isn't. This treatment of you is *very* different from that of a friend you trust who is giving you some blunt advice.

Step 3: Let yourself heal. You know you felt angry. You also may have felt defensive, fearful, guilty, self-blaming, depressed, or other emotions.

- Do *not* deny or act on your feelings. Just feel them.

- Let yourself *feel* what you feel. Let the feelings come—and go.

- Give yourself the time and space to do this.

Step 4: Get back to your life. The other person was a nuisance. A bump in the road. Don't give them any more time or energy now. Focus on your own life, activities, and people.

Something unexpected may happen: by the time you get back to your life, you may end up *feeling sorry* for the other person.

But even if you don't, you're no longer giving them power by staying angry at them. Your anger—and theirs—are no longer in charge of you. *You* are.

Grieving

Sometimes, you may be angry because of something much bigger than a grudge. You may be *grieving* the loss of someone, or something, you love. This might come from the death of someone you love, or the loss of a good job, or the loss of your youth—anything that means a *lot* to you. You might grieve over the fact that you can't change things you think are unfair. Or that you can't control situations—or people—you want to control.

Here's how grieving relates to anger. The grieving steps are the *same* as the four steps of "Letting Go of Grudges in General," in the section above. You could call grieving "Letting Go of Someone or Something You Love." When you lose someone or something, you go through all the same steps—with one difference.

The difference is: before you go through Denial—which is Step 1 under "Letting Go of Grudges in General"—the first step in grieving is *Shock*. Shock means you can neither *think* nor *feel*. Both your *mind* and your *guts* are *numb*. Once the reality sinks in, you get out of Shock and go into Denial—and follow all the other steps in "Letting Go of Grudges in General."

If you don't grieve, you stay *stuck*—and *angry*—in the same way you would if you don't let go of grudges. Grieving lets you *feel and then get past* your losses, so you can reach Step 4: Taking back control of your life.

In Skill #1, you decided both you and the other person were willing to talk things over. In Skill #2, you went to the person you're angry at. In Skill #3, you paid attention to their feelings (as well as your own). In Skill #4, you found something in common with them. In Skill #5, you depersonalized the situation. In Skill #6, you got to the real issues. In Skill #7, you let go of your grudge—in the short term, the long term, and in cases where the other person would not cooperate.

These seven skills help you take charge of your anger. *And* of your life.

Next, we'll take a different look at the stories you read at the beginning of the book. This time, we'll see how to deal with the same situations *using the seven skills*—the *adult woman's* way to deal with anger.

ASK YOURSELF...

1. Think of one person you like to hold a grudge against.

2. What do you like about holding this grudge?

3. What would it "cost" you—that is, what would you lose—by letting go of this grudge?

4. How aware are you of the "hole" that the grudge helps "fill"?

5. What other ways do you try to "fill" the "hole"?

6. What might you gain by letting go of this grudge?

11

Applying the Seven Skills to Our Opening Stories

ow, we'll look again at the women's stories we started with. You'll see how to use the skills in each story. Each story has its own section:

- Jealousy   76
- No control over what happens to you   80
- Being questioned   84
- Date-raped   88
- Having to be strong   92
- Wanting something   95
- Unfairness at work   97
- Your kids   99
- Grief   102
- Domestic violence   104
- How to Interview a Therapist or Helper   108
- Giving up addictions   109
- Incest   112
- Pornography   115

Jealousy

I knew he was going out on me. He denied it, but I knew. You know how you just know stuff like that? The more he said he wasn't, the more sure I was that he was.

But here's the thing. I work all day. I have no time to chase him around to see who he's with or what he's doing. When I get home, there's the kids to take care of. I can't track him down when he says he's out with his buddies.

So I have no proof. At least, none that I can show him. But he's been staying out later than usual. He doesn't push me for sex like he used to. He suddenly decides one day that he should take care of the checkbook instead of me.

And you know what else? He's gotten a lot nicer. To me. I know this sounds crazy, but that's what really proves it to me. He's nicer because he's guilty.

So I'm angry. Real angry. What does he think I am, his maid? Not thin enough? Not young enough? Not sexy enough? Who can be sexy with three kids and a lot of bills? That jerk thinks I'm too stupid to catch on. He thinks he can go out on me and get away with it. I'm angry enough to divorce him.

But there's the kids. He makes a lot more money than me. I'd have to get a cheaper place to live. One month of him skipping child support, and the kids and I would be out in the street.

And then there's custody. The kids are close to him. He could afford to stay here and keep the kids in the same school. I could lose the kids if I divorced him.

And if I did get custody, or even if I just left, the kids would hate my guts. They'd blame me for breaking up the family.

So, yeah, I'm angry. And you know what I do about it? Nothing. I smile, act the same as always. I act like nothing's wrong. You know why? Because it's easier for everyone that way.

That's why I like the Valium so much. It takes the edge off. It helps me get through the day.

In this case:

Skill #1: Decide (1) if *you're* ready to talk about it, and (2) if the other person is ready.
If *you're* the woman speaking, it's clear you're *not* ready to talk it over with him. It sounds like he isn't ready to talk it over, either. Skill #1 won't work here. But you can still use the other steps to help you.

Skill #2: Talk to the person you're angry at (and keep everyone else out of it).
You can't use this skill without Skill #1.

Skill #3: Pay attention to their feelings (as well as your own).
This won't work without Skill #1.

Skill #4: Find something in common.
Neither will this. You have the marriage and children in common, but he doesn't sound willing to resolve anything.

Skill #5: Depersonalize the situation.
This is the first skill you can use in this case. You are *not* to blame for *any* of his actions. His actions are because of *him*—not you. This is *very* important for you to know, because too many women blame themselves when their husbands or boyfriends go out on them, lie, or betray them in other ways.

Skill #6: Get to the *real* issue(s).
You have several real issues here:

1. He's giving you Two-Faced Anger—acting nice towards you, giving you "good" reasons to take over the checkbook, but going out on you behind your back. You *must stop* "caving in" and "taking" it.

2. He's also using Self-Centered Anger on you. He does what he wants, even though it hurts you and the kids.

3. You're suffering from your own Drinking/Drugging Anger. Valium is part of the trap you're caught in. You'll see more about this, below.

4. *He's* responsible for what he's doing. You're *not*. But, at the same time, *you* are in charge of how you react to your anger—for your sake *and* for your kids' sake.

5. You think the Valium helps you get through each day. But the truth is that it makes you numb, passive, and unable to take good care of your kids *or* yourself. In this situation, Valium is a form of *denial.* It stops you from thinking. It shuts off your judgment. It keeps you in a fog. It keeps you stuck with him.

6. You risk getting addicted to Valium. Addiction makes you even more of a slave to Valium—and to your husband.

7. Valium is part of the *trap* you're caught in. Your anger is trying to tell you something—but the Valium keeps you from listening.

8. You have to give up the Valium—and every other "medicine" or substance that lets you hide from reality and from your feelings. Twelve-step programs, counseling, and other treatment programs can make this easier.

9. Your anger is trying to tell you that you deserve better treatment than your husband is giving you.

10. Your anger is trying to tell you that you can't keep depending on him—in either an emotional way *or* a practical way.

11. Your anger is trying to say that you need to get information and do some planning—about training for a job, working to support yourself and your kids, finding a babysitter or daycare for the kids while you're working, and other steps to become more independent.

   Once you're more independent, you'll have a much better chance of getting custody, if that becomes an issue. *Even if you stay with him,* the more independent you are, the less you'll be at the mercy of what he does. And the more control you'll have over your own life.

12. Your anger is trying to tell you that you should get some counseling—with your husband, or by yourself. Counseling will help you take the steps you need to take to become more independent. If he goes also and the relationship improves, both of you gain. If not, you will gain by working on yourself.

13. Whether you stay with him "forever" or not, you can take all these steps *now,* while you're still with him. If nothing else, his financial and practical support will make it easier for you to take steps *now* towards becoming more independent.

Skill #7: Drop the grudge.

If counseling helps the relationship, he treats you the way he should, and you can trust him, you can drop the grudge by enjoying his support and loyalty. The steps in "Letting Go of Grudges in General" will help.

If counseling doesn't help, the more independent you get, the less he will matter—and the easier it will be for you to drop your grudge. The section on "How to Drop the Grudge So You Can Act *Now*" will help you take the steps towards independence—while you're still with him for practical and financial reasons.

If you take the steps you need towards real independence *now,* while you're still with him, you can drop the grudge because you know you're going in the direction of being able to take care of yourself—and the kids—*with or without* him. Your own independence will make it easier to drop the grudge because *you* have more control of your own life.

No control over what happens to you

Nobody understands this. Not even my doctor. Food makes me sick to my stomach. The sight of it. The way it looks. The way it smells. But the worst part is the feel of it in my mouth. It makes me gag.

I've never told this to anyone before. It makes me gag to even say it.

But the feel of food in my mouth is just like when I was little. The babysitter stuck something in my mouth. I was terrified. I felt like I was suffocating. Drowning. The slimy feel in my mouth and throat.

I had no idea at the time what was happening. I didn't have the words to even know what I felt. Now I can say I felt terrified. But I also felt dirty. Ashamed. Disgusted. He had done a disgusting thing to me. I was too little to know what was going on. But I felt all these ways.

And that's what food feels like. Every time I put food in my mouth, it feels like that. Even the smell of food does it to me.

Everyone tries to get me to eat. Some come straight out and tell me to eat. Others are sneakier. They ask if I'm hungry, or they eat something and look at me as if I'll get hungry from watching.

Or they'll lecture me about all the dangers of not eating. How all my organs will shut down. My guts, my liver, my kidneys. My doctor does this. But he doesn't understand. Talking about my organs does the same thing as the food. It all makes me feel like throwing up.

It all makes me mad. I get angry at the way they think they can talk me into wanting to eat. Like I'm still a child. I get angry that they don't even know how I feel. I get mad at myself for not being able to tell them.

Anyway, I found a way to get my mind off the whole subject. I work out—as many hours a day as I can.

In this case:

Skill #1: Decide (1) if _you're_ ready to talk about it, and (2) if the other person is ready.
If you're the woman with anorexia, it sounds like you _think_ you don't want to talk about it, but you also wish you could. It also sounds like there are many people, not just one, you feel torn about talking to. You're unsure whether you're ready or not, and you don't think any of the others are ready to hear you.

You have a choice here. Because you _wish_ you could talk about it—even though you don't think you can—you _might_ want to try talking to the person who, you think, would be the most open to hearing you. If you try with this person, there's a good chance they _will_ be ready to listen, because they want to help. The key here is to pick someone who will _listen to you_ more than they will try to _talk to_ you.

The person may be a friend, a teacher, a religious leader, a family member, or someone else you trust.

If you can think of such a person, we can assume that the answers to (1) and (2) are _yes_, and that Skill #1 will work.

Skill #2: Talk to the person you're angry at (and keep everyone else out of it).
Once you pick the person who you think will _listen_ instead of _talk,_ keep it between just the two of you. Go to this person and tell them, "I'm angry about this food thing. If you're willing to listen, and let me do most of the talking, I think you can help me."

This is different from most cases where you're angry at a specific person. In this case, the other person wants to help you, and is trying in ways that don't work for you. But because they _want_ to help, they're very likely to listen to you.

Skill #3: Pay attention to their feelings (as well as your own).
Tell them you know that they're worried about you, and that they're trying to help. Do _not_ talk yet about why they're not really helping! For this step, focus on letting them know that you realize they mean well.

Skill #4: Find something in common.
Both you and they want you to feel better.

Skill #5: Depersonalize the situation.
They're worried about you, so of course it's easy to take this personally. But they're worried, fearful, angry, and upset at the _anorexia_—not at you, the person. This is an important difference.

The anorexia is *not* "you." It is an illness, like cancer or the flu. And it's also a *symptom*—of the abuse you suffered, and the impact the abuse had on you. The illness and the symptom—*not you*—are the problem.

The molestation you suffered as a child was *not because* of you. It was because of a sick person who picked you *only because* you were there, you were little, and it was easy for *them*. It was *their* fault. *Not* yours.

Skill #6: Get to the *real* issue(s).
You have a number of real issues going on:

1. You're getting Two-Faced Anger from everyone. They think they're trying to help you, but you *feel* it as pressure. You can't stand the way they *force* "help" on you—yet you also *need* some help.

   You're going to have to separate "forced" help from *real* help. You need help—but on *your* terms.

2. You have Rigid Anger towards everyone. You're desperately trying to control your own behavior *and* everyone's reaction to you. Your Rigid Anger is making your other problems worse.

3. Even if you've had counseling, the abuse you endured may never have been dealt with or even mentioned. *Many eating-disorder therapists do not even ask whether you were ever molested!* This is true *even though most women with eating disorders were sexually abused as infants and/or children.* If you've had counseling but still are trapped in an eating disorder, *stop blaming yourself.*

4. One reason you're angry—*and* afraid to talk—is that even if the other person is open and willing to listen more than talk, they may not believe what you say about the abuse. Or they may not want to hear it. *You already know this.*

5. You also know that bringing it out in the open could cause problems in your family.

6. You need, and deserve, help *in dealing with the abuse and its effects on you.*

7. There are ways to get this help without necessarily wrecking your whole family. But the trap you feel is that it will change at least some of the relationships you have with some family members. That's why you need help—no one can get out of this kind of trap by themselves.

8. Just _being heard_ by the person you're talking to is a huge help and a beginning for you. Your goal is to practice, so that you'll be able to talk about these issues with a counselor. A counselor who is both _willing_ and _able_ to help you with the childhood _molestation_, as well as with the problems you have with _food_.

9. With help from this person, or by yourself, you need to find a counselor to talk with about the abuse you endured. _Tell_ the counselor this. Even though counselors should, they don't always connect anorexia with abuse. And they usually don't realize that the taste or feel of food connects to the abuse issues. Odd as this may seem, you'll have to help your counselor help you.

Skill #7: Drop the grudge.

The anger you felt—towards the people who tried to get you to eat—was real. But it wasn't really about them. It was more about your general feeling of being trapped. Along with counseling, the section under "Grieving" will help you let go of these feelings.

Being questioned

Sometimes my boyfriend makes me so mad. Things will be just fine, and then, bam! He starts asking me all these questions.

Today, I get home from work, and right away he wants to know if Rick, a guy I work with, was there today. That made me mad.

What difference does it make whether Rick was there or not? He's just one of my co-workers. He's this computer nerd, and my boyfriend knows it. So I asked him why he wanted to know.

Well, that set him right off. He starts yelling about me keeping secrets from him. He goes on and on, saying stuff about me liking Rick, sneaking out with him for lunch, stuff like that. I finally told him yes, Rick was there. So then he goes, "See? And how come you asked why I wanted to know? I have a right to know which guys you're hanging out with!"

It didn't do any good to remind him that Rick is just another guy I work with. Or that I'm working, not hanging out. I reminded him that Rick is just a computer nerd. That still didn't do any good. He wanted to know where I had lunch, who was there, stuff like that. He just went on and on.

I was so mad! But it doesn't do any good to tell him that. He just gets louder and has more questions. I felt like slapping him in the face and walking out.

But I did what I always do when he gets like this. I told him no man could measure up to him. I rubbed up against him. We wound up having sex.

Which made me even angrier.

In this case:

Skill #1: Decide (1) if *you're* ready to talk about it, and (2) if the other person is ready.
If you were this woman, it sounds like you're ready—and trying!—to talk things over. It sounds like your boyfriend wants to talk more than listen. But it may be worth *trying* to use these skills with him. Let's start out *assuming* that he, too, is ready.

Skill #2: Talk to the person you're angry at (and keep everyone else out of it).
Talk only to your boyfriend about this. Keep your friends and everyone else out of it.

Skill #3: Pay attention to their feelings (as well as your own).
Start this conversation at a time when you're getting along well with each other. Do *not* try these steps when he is questioning you or getting upset in other ways. Remember that in this step, you're focusing on *his* feelings, not yours.

Start out by telling him, "I want to talk about things that bother you. You seem worried that I'm interested in Rick, or that I go to lunch with him, or that I like him."

Skill #4: Find something in common.
Go immediately to what you and your boyfriend have in common. "I want to talk this over, because I love you and we have a good relationship."

Skill #5: Depersonalize the situation.
Your boyfriend *thinks* you like Rick. But this has more to do with his own fears than with what you're doing. *He* doesn't know this yet. And you *can't tell him* this yet. But *you* know this is true.

When you know this, it's easier for you not to take it personally. This might help you stay calmer while you're talking—and listening.

Skill #6: Get to the *real* issue(s).
On the surface, the real issue is that your boyfriend questions you when he should trust you. But you *also* must find out which of two *underlying* real issues is going on:

1. Your boyfriend may be afraid of losing you *and* willing to go with you to a counselor to get help with his fears. In this case, talking things over (including with the counselor) should help stop his questioning.

He's showing you Self-Centered Anger—and instead of giving in, you must insist on him going to counseling to deal with it.

OR

2. Your boyfriend may be afraid of losing you *and* trying to *control* you by tracking who you know, who you spend time with, what men you talk to, and who else is in your life. He may want to *limit* the number of people you see. He may want to *remove* from your life, one by one, every friend and family member you love and enjoy. He may want to *isolate* and *trap* you, and make *himself* the only person in your life. His questioning—and his *anger*— may be only the *tools* he uses to trap you in a long, ever-tightening imprisonment.

You've also got other real issues:

3. You're working against yourself by using Two-Faced Anger against him. You act like everything is fine, and keep your anger inside. You make it easy for him to say he "didn't know" you were upset.

4. Your boyfriend is using Rigid Anger to control you. You have to decide whether it's because of #1 or #2, above. If it's #2, using these skills in talking with him will only make things worse—*which is how he's been reacting so far,* when you try to talk and reason with him. It's clear that his goals are to *trap and control* you.

    You must take these steps to get more independent—and to leave him:

    ▪ Find a friend, relative, or shelter where you can stay—*without* him knowing where you are. If you're afraid of him, get information about "orders of protection" or "restraining orders."

    ▪ Based on the information, decide whether you are better off with or without a restraining order.

    ▪ Sometimes restraining orders work. Other times they make the guy angrier. One big benefit about restraining orders, though, is that they make the man's *presence* illegal. He can be arrested for *being near you,* even if he hasn't hit you yet.

- Without a restraining order, he can be arrested only *after* hurting you.

- Save all the money you can (or, if you're not working, find work). Put your money in *your own* bank account, with *only your* name and signature. Keep this account, and the money, *secret.*

- Find, and use, counseling resources available to you.

- When you can afford it, get your own place. Keep your address, phone number, workplace, and all other information about you *unlisted* and unavailable to him.

- Hang up if he calls. If he shows up, keep the door locked, say nothing through the door, and call the police—a restraining order will be very helpful here. Warn Human Resources and Security at work about him—tell them he's dangerous, and let them know if you have a restraining order.

Skill #7: Drop the grudge.
If he's just insecure, and the conversation helps, it's easy to drop the grudge. If he's trying to control you, it will be easier to drop your grudge *after* you're more independent and you get him out of your life.

The steps in "How to Drop the Grudge When the Other Person Wants to *Get* You" will help. So will your independence from him. The "Grieving" section will help you deal with your loss of the good parts of the relationship—or, of the *belief* that it was good, or of the *hope* that it would get better.

Date-raped

I would never have believed this could happen to me. But there I was, at a party with a bunch of my friends, and the next thing I know, I wake up in a strange room. I'm alone in some strange bed, and I've peed all over myself. My head feels weird, like I'm in a fog or a dream. My clothes are all over the floor. At the time, I didn't even think about my car—which, it turned out, was still at my friend's house where the party was.

I was terrified. I didn't even know where I was. Nothing looked familiar. I couldn't think clearly. I couldn't remember anyone's phone number. I got more and more afraid by the minute. My heart was pounding and racing. My head was so fuzzy. My whole crotch area really, really hurt.

I was scared. Then I realized I'd been raped. I vomited. I felt sick. I wanted to crawl right out of my body. I felt dirty, filthy. I threw up again.

I took a shower. Wanted to wash everything off of me. Over and over. Wanted to shower to make me clean, clean, clean. Maybe it would also clear my head. I got dressed. Then I realized I should call the police.

It turns out I was only a few miles from where I live. A neighborhood I'd never been in before. I'd been drugged—one of those date-rape drugs. Never tasted anything. Never saw or smelled anything. Can't remember anything after talking to a bunch of people at the party.

I'd been raped, all right. Sodomized, too. God knows by who, or how many guys, or how many times. Thank God I didn't get pregnant, on top of everything else. No signs of STD. At least, not so far.

But the shower had washed away the evidence. No way to prove who'd done what. Even my friends could only guess. They were all so drunk or high or stoned at the party that no one remembered when I left or who with.

I can't even tell you whether I'm angry. I understand what happened. I know it's not my fault. I know I should be angry.

But I don't feel angry. What I feel like is . . . well, I feel like a piece of dirt. Like no matter how many showers I take, nothing will ever make me clean. I feel dirty all over.

I dream about it every night. One dream I have over and over—I'm in the shower, and so much water washes over me that I dissolve, just disappear, right there in the shower. All gone, along with the dirt.

But I can't say I'm angry. I'm just a lot more private now. More careful about who I talk to and where I go. And I stay away from parties.

In this case:

Skill #1: Decide (1) if *you're* ready to talk about it, and (2) if the other person is ready.
You *think* you don't want to talk about it. But your feelings, thoughts, bad dreams, and isolation mean you *need* to. In this case, the "other person" is not there.

But you *can* talk with someone who can help you by listening. And you *can* take steps to help yourself.

Skill #2: Talk to the person you're angry at (and keep everyone else out of it).
The "other person"—your attacker—is unknown to you. This makes you angrier. And more in need of talking with someone who's *on your side*.

Skill #3: Pay attention to their feelings (as well as your own).
In this case, *only your feelings* matter.

Skill #4: Find something in common.
There is no such thing in this situation.

Skill #5: Depersonalize the situation.
You *can't* depersonalize what the rapist did to you. It was *extremely* personal. But you *can* remember that it was also *anonymous*. He picked you as a target, *but not because it was you,* and *not because of* you. He was a predator. He took advantage of your *presence*—the fact that you were *there*. You had a *right* to be there—and to be *safe* there. He violated you because you were "there"—but *you* were not the cause of the violation. *He* was.

In another way, you've depersonalized *too much*. That is, you're losing touch with your feelings and yourself. That's why you understand—in your head—that you "should" be angry, and yet you *don't feel*—in your body—angry. You need help getting back in touch with yourself.

Skill #6: Get to the *real* issue(s).
You have a number of real issues:

1. The predator who drugged, kidnapped, and attacked you used Rigid Anger on you. You couldn't defend yourself while you were drugged.

   But *now* you can refuse to let him rule you. You *can*—and *must*—take steps to regain control of your life.

2. You were *drugged*—with something that had the same effects as the anesthesia doctors use on patients having surgery. During surgery, patients are monitored *because these types of drugs can*

kill them or cause brain damage. During surgery, patients are monitored constantly for allergic reactions, breathing difficulties, and other potential problems. Your attacker and rapist put you at the same types of risk *without* any of these safety precautions.

3. You were *kidnapped*—forced to a strange place against your will or, at best, without your awareness (much less your consent). You were *made* unconscious, then *dragged*—unconscious—to a strange place, attacked, and left alone. All this time, you were at the mercy of a powerful anesthetic drug that could have hurt your brain and central nervous system.

4. You were *raped* and *sodomized*. Multiple times. The physical, emotional, and psychological effects on you are only *beginning.* Emotionally, you're stuck at the "shock" stage of grieving.

5. This triple or quadruple crime is taken *much too lightly*—not only by the police, but also by society in general, including your friends.

   Date-rape drugs are treated as "recreational"—some people even take them for "fun."

6. Women are being seen, more and more, as *things* instead of as *people.* The attacker used you as a warm version of an inflatable sex-toy doll. *He did not see you as a human being.*

7. Your numbness and isolation are signs of *post-traumatic stress*, which includes—but is not limited to—depression and anger. Your anger—combined with feeling helpless about the whole thing— can be a source of energy *if* you're able to feel it. But it takes work, and help, to get past your numbness. The section on "Drop the Grudge So You Can Act *Now*" will help get you started.

8. Without help, you risk staying stuck in depression, anger, and other negative—and dangerous—feelings. Many untreated victims get into drugs, alcohol, and other self-destructive behaviors. Some eventually commit suicide.

9. You *have the chance* to regain control of your life—instead of letting the predator lower its quality *or* completely take it away from you.

10. You need counseling. No matter how much you "understand" in your mind what happened, you need to get into your feelings. The

section on "Grieving" will help you get started. But a good counselor can help you truly heal.

11. You *must* push for justice. You can't let him get away with "getting" you—and with controlling your life, which he's still doing now. Get friends to help you find out who the perpetrator may have been. Find out what pieces of information different people have. Get witnesses. Get support from the police, even if you need your friends there for emotional support when you do. Get help piecing together different people's bits of information. Make sure all witnesses and suspects are questioned. Find out where to get legal help for free or low cost—and *get* the legal help. Make sure arrests are made. Press charges. Push for enough information to bring suspects to trial. Get yourself ready to be a good witness.

    Get counseling to help you do all of this. You *deserve* to stand up for yourself in court. You *deserve* to have the legal system work for you.

    The attacker used Rigid Anger to take over control of your life. You want that control *back*.

12. You must be more protective and loving towards yourself. Start with a counselor who you feel comfortable with. And who you trust.

    You don't have to stay away from all parties. But you *do* have to make sure you stay in control of yourself, your brain, what you eat and drink, and who you're with.

    This is important. It's also sad. One of the things you're grieving is the loss of innocence, of trust in people. This doesn't mean you can't trust anyone. It means you have to be careful about *who* you trust. Which is still a loss. The "Grieving" section will help.

Skill #7: Drop the grudge.
You don't even have the "benefit" knowing which specific person to hold a grudge against. Instead, you have a general, overall feeling of being down—on yourself, on everyone you know, on life. The section on "How Drop the Grudge When the Other Person Wants to *Get* You" will help. So will the section on "Grieving."

Counseling will make all of this much easier. But with or without counseling, you can still take the steps to get your life back.

Having to be strong

I left home when I was 12. Couldn't get along with my folks. My father kept trying to control my life, and my mother just followed whatever he said. He wanted me to be like her—no guts, no backbone, no life of her own. She was just a servant to him.

I think now that I was too strong for my father. He knew he couldn't control me. I even stood up to him when I was five and he tried to touch me wrong. I told him I'd tell the police if he tried again. Five years old! I had to be strong, with the way things were at home.

So when I left, some friends said I could stay at their houses. But the parents always kicked me out for no reason at all. After a while, I got real angry about having to count on other people. It was too much like living with my parents.

So that's how I decided to work the streets. Easy money. Not hard work, like cleaning people's houses. I wasn't like some of the other girls, who got talked into it, or got forced into it. I made the decision myself.

I also knew I didn't need no guy to protect me. I could take care of myself. And, for a while, it worked. But some of the customers were scary. One guy punched me so hard he knocked a tooth out. Another beat me with the handle of his gun, for no reason at all.

So then this fancy guy tells me I'll be dead if I don't have a man to protect me. I knew he was right. So I let him do that for me. And he was real nice to me. For a while.

But it turned out I was just another one of the girls to him. He was just another guy trying to control me.

But it don't do no good to get angry, you know. He don't care. My customers don't care. Even I don't care! I just light up or shoot or smoke or whatever's around.

And then I'm not so angry for a while.

In this case:

Skill #1: Decide (1) if *you're* ready to talk about it, and (2) if the other person is ready.
You might want to talk to your "guy," but it doesn't sound like you think he'd be ready. It also doesn't sound like it would do much good to talk to your customers. You're angry—but at the world, not just a specific person. There's no one to use Skill #1 with.

But there *are* steps you can take to help yourself:

Skill #2: Talk to the person you're angry at (and keep everyone else out of it).
There's no particular person you're angry at. But you can still get help for your anger.

Skill #3: Pay attention to their feelings (as well as your own).
In this case, *your* feelings are all that matter.

Skill #4: Find something in common.
This skill doesn't work here.

Skill #5: Depersonalize the situation.
You already know that your father's need for control, and his attempt to molest you, are *not* your fault. You might be able to learn something by accepting *some* responsibility for your friends' parents having trouble with you living with them. But one thing working *against* you in this area is that you depersonalize *too much.* You had to depersonalize to be strong. But you've done it so "well" that you've lost touch with your feelings—and with yourself.

Skill #6: Get to the *real* issue(s).
You have several real issues:

1. Your father, customers, and "guy" all used Rigid Anger against you.

2. You're suffering from your own Acted-Out Anger, Rigid Anger, and Drinking/Drugging Anger. Your self-destructive life can be seen as acting out your anger—against yourself. Your extreme need for control over your life can been seen as Rigid Anger. And the drugs you use are part of your Drinking/Drugging Anger. All of them are hurting you.

3. You've done a good job staying alive—so far. Now, you want more. Beyond just staying alive, you want to *enjoy* life. You want your life to *mean* something. You want to get beyond merely *surviving.*

You're also at risk of *not* staying alive. The drugs themselves could kill you. AIDS or Hepatitis C—from using needles—could kill you. Your everyday life could kill you.

4. The drugs numb you. Your anger is trying to tell you to get on with your life, but the drugs make *nothing matter.* The drugs take away all your energy and focus. They stop you from growing and changing. They keep you locked in anger, fighting the world—and hurting yourself. They also make you more and more depressed. The depression leads to more drugs—and you're caught in a circle you can't get out of. You lose control of your own life.

5. You're independent at heart. Before the drugs take that away from you, you must *build* on it. You can get help from local community agencies. But *you* have to take the steps and do the work:

   ■ You have to get off the drugs before you can grow or do anything else. Treatment centers can help. So can 12-step programs.

   ■ You need help taking care of yourself *physically.* This means everything from getting food to eat, to showering every day and wearing clean clothes.

   ■ You have to get training for work. This may be in school or through social service agencies. A *real* job is the key to your real independence.

   ■ You have to get help with the *people* side of work, as well as the technical details of a job. You have to learn how to get along with others. You have to be able to hear what a real boss says—*without* seeing them boss as a controlling father or another "guy."

   ■ You have to find friends—real friends who care about how you feel, and who you care about.

Skill #7: Drop the grudge.
Your grudge is towards life in general. It includes being angry at yourself. The section on "How to Drop the Grudge So You Can Act *Now* " will help you rebuild your independence and take the steps you need to take. The section on "Grieving" will help you let go of the pain you've had.

And your steps towards independence will give you real control of your life.

Wanting something

I didn't start out walking into a store for the purpose of stealing. One day, there I was, getting a pack of cigarettes. While the cashier was breaking a roll of coins, I saw this glittery thing. It was a little change purse, hanging on a hook. It was just there. So I grabbed it and folded it up in my free hand.

She didn't see. I paid for my cigarettes and left.

The next time, I was in a bigger store, and there was this loose pile of underwear. I grabbed a few panties and stuffed them in my shirt.

After a while, I'd picked up enough clothes to have a whole new wardrobe. All for free!

And you know, I deserve these things. Other people have the money to buy stuff. It's not my fault that I don't. I didn't have any rich parents to buy me nice things. I don't have any rich boyfriend, either.

And when you see what kinds of crooks are running the companies, why should I pay for anything? They have more money than I do. And everyone else I know.

So I don't really think of it as stealing. It's more like, you know, just getting what I need. So when I end up in jail, it makes me furious. How come everyone else can get away with it, but not me?

In this case:

Skill #1: Decide (1) if *you're* ready to talk about it, and (2) if the other person is ready.
Your anger is inside you. It's not aimed at anyone in particular. It's aimed at *everyone.* Even though you're not angry at one specific individual, you still can use some of these skills to help yourself.

Skill #2: Talk to the person you're angry at (and keep everyone else out of it).
This skill doesn't apply here.

Skill #3: Pay attention to their feelings (as well as your own).
In this case, *your* feelings are all that's important.

Skill #4: Find something in common.
This skill doesn't work here.

Skill #5: Depersonalize the situation.
You're already *too good* at depersonalizing. You don't see others as real people. You think you're entitled to whatever's out there. You think *nobody* earns what they have, so you don't have to, either. You think *nothing* is fair in life.

But you get in trouble when you get caught. This isn't working for you.

Skill #6: Get to the *real* issue(s).
You have several real issues:

1. You're showing Self-Centered Anger. You steal what you want, no matter whose it is. You think you "deserve" whatever you want. You see the world the way an infant does—you as the center of the universe, the only important person, and others as "props" to serve you. This view is understandable for an infant. But it's selfish, immature, and irresponsible for a grown-up.

2. You make up excuses for your actions. Would you accept these excuses from a person who stole something from *you*?

3. Your stealing is about *more* than the stuff you steal. It's about not getting enough love or caring or other good feelings, from other people. You think you have to "steal" to get the love you need—and deserve. You think you can't get love and attention the "honest" way. Counseling can help you with this. So can the section on "Grieving."

4. You need some help caring about other people. If you cared more about other people, they'd care more about you. *And* you could start caring more about yourself as a person.

Skill #7: Drop the grudge.
The section on "Letting Go of Grudges in General" can help you. The more you give—emotionally—to others, the less grudging you'll feel. Of course, you have to make sure that you love and care for people who are *good* for you. Within this limit, caring for others will help you get rid of your Self-Centered Anger—and reclaim control of your life.

Unfairness at work

I've had this job for three years now. My boss knows I do a good job.

But this new woman starts working there, and for some reason she starts bad-mouthing me. She tells everyone that I just slack off when I should be working. Who does she think she is? She really made me mad.

But the next thing I know, my boss calls me in. He starts asking me questions about how I'm spending my time, whether there's a way to get more done in the same amount of time, things like that. I know that's because of what this new woman has been saying.

Why does my boss believe her, when I'm the one who's been doing a good job for three years? It makes me furious!

In this case:

Skill #1: Decide (1) if *you're* ready to talk about it, and (2) if the other person is ready.
You're ready to talk to your boss, and your boss sounds willing to listen. The answer to both questions in Skill #1 is "yes."

Skill #2: Talk to the person you're angry at (and keep everyone else out of it).
This *must* stay between you and your boss. Say nothing to the new woman or anyone else at work. Not even your friends at work.

Skill #3: Pay attention to their feelings (as well as your own).
Based on his questions, it's fair to say your boss is at least curious about your work and your time management. He may even be concerned about both. You can start out by saying that, based on what he's asked you, it sounds like he's got some questions or concerns about your work.

Skill #4: Find something in common.
Both you and your boss want you to do a good job. Both of you want things to go well at work.

Skill #5: Depersonalize the situation.

So far, your boss has done a good job of asking questions about your work. He has *not* dragged in the name of the new woman. He has *not* made personal remarks about you.

You want to do the same—stick to work, stick to what you're doing, stick to how you manage time. Do *not* make accusations about the "new woman" starting rumors about you. Do *not* act defensive, as if you're being accused of something. Help your boss stay focused on work performance issues.

If your boss starts talking about what the "new employee" said, or starts accusing you of things or making assumptions, stay calm and bring him back to what *you* are doing on the job.

Skill #6: Get to the *real* issue(s).

You have a few real issues taking place here:

1. You're using Two-Faced Anger here. You're *assuming* that the new co-worker told the boss something about you. You're *assuming* that boss believed her. And you don't even have any facts! You're jumping to conclusions—and assuming you have an "enemy"—before you know what's going on. You feel defensive, and you want to "get even," about something that *may not have even happened.*

2. The most important issue is what your boss thinks of your work. This may—or may *not*—have anything to do with the new co-worker.

3. You're *assuming* the new employee said bad things about you. Don't jump to conclusions. Wait until the boss says something about it. If he doesn't, leave her out of the discussion. If he does, you can bring him back to what he knows about your work. You also can help him separate "what a co-worker said" from how your work really is.

4. Be open to your boss's input. He may want you to make changes or improvements. Remember that this is about your *work*—not about what the new employee may or may not have said.

5. If the boss's input seems unfair, you can tell him. You can stick to your work behavior, how you do your work, and what the results are. You can avoid making it personal. You can help your boss do the same.

Skill #7: Drop the grudge.

Be neutral about the new employee. You don't have to be her friend, but there's no need to create enemies, either. If she seems "out to get you," the section on "How to Drop the Grudge When the Other Person Wants to *Get* You" will help.

If your boss has problems with your work, there's no need for grudges, either. Just focus on the work. If your boss is being unfair, stick to the work issues to resolve the problem. The section on "Letting Go of Grudges in General" can help.

Your kids

My boy had just turned two. I couldn't let him out of my sight for three seconds. He opens everything up, tries to drink out of any cups or glasses he can reach, and keeps turning on the water faucet. He loves to play with electric outlets, and when I smack his hand and tell him "no," he just laughs and runs away.

One day, when I'm sick with the flu, he climbs up on the entertainment center, gets on top of the TV, and tries to push the TV to the floor. If I hadn't come running in right then, he could've ended up with the TV on top of him.

I'd had enough! I grabbed him, and he's so strong that he's hanging onto the TV. I had trouble pulling him off. I was afraid the damn thing would fall on both of us. The whole time, he's yelling, "No! No!" It was like my whole purpose in life was to watch after him!

I was sick, my head was pounding, and I was afraid the TV would hurt him. But I was also angry. SO angry that I just started hitting him. I couldn't stop. I heard him screaming, "Stop, Mama! Stop, Mama!" I was so mad I couldn't stop myself.

His little voice sounded so far away. I was furious. I hit him and kept hitting, hitting. I hit him until he suddenly got quiet.

Real quiet.

In this case:

Skill #1: Decide (1) if *you're* ready to talk about it, and (2) if the other person is ready.

You clearly weren't ready to talk about it. Even if you were, a two-year-old could not keep up his end of the conversation. You'd have to use these skills for yourself, so you could deal with him in a way that worked with two-year-olds.

Skill #2: Talk to the person you're angry at (and keep everyone else out of it).
This would have helped, *if* you used the skills to work with his age level.

Skill #3: Pay attention to their feelings (as well as your own).
You dealt *only* with *your own* feelings. You did not make room for his. It's easy to see why—he was so into his own feelings, that you felt there was no room for *yours*. But as the adult, you're supposed to be more understanding than your two-year-old.

Skill #4: Find something in common.
What you had in common was a mother-child relationship. Hopefully, you also shared love and fun. But at this crucial moment, all you *let* the two of you share was the fact that *both* of you were too wrapped up in your own feelings to pay attention to the other's. Emotionally, you *both* were two years old at that moment.

Skill #5: Depersonalize the situation.
You were *way* too personally involved. You took your two-year-old's behavior as a challenge or an insult—as if he were an adult. You were just as wrapped up in your *own* feelings as he was in his. You didn't put a S-P-A-C-E between your feelings and your actions. Even though adults are supposed to be able to get *past* their feelings, to help their children, and to keep their children safe.

Skill #6: Get to the *real* issue(s).
You have a number of *serious* real issues going on:

1. You used Acted-Out Anger on your two-year-old, in hitting him.

2. You used Irresponsible Anger, focusing *only* on that moment, with no thought for the *results* of what you were doing.

3. You used Self-Centered Anger, being so wrapped up in *your own* anger, and in expecting him to act like a grown-up.

4. You used Two-Faced Anger, beating him up because you were worried about his safety!

5. You used Rigid Anger, using physical abuse to control him.

6. No matter what you *meant* to do, the fact is that you *beat* your two-year-old son until he was physically disabled, brain-damaged, or dead.

7. You *didn't* put a S-P-A-C-E between what you *felt* and what you *did*. You did FEELDO. Everyone *feels* the feelings you felt. But *adults* are supposed to separate these *feelings* from their *actions*.

8. You used the child as an *outlet,* or *target,* for your anger and frustrations. Even though part of your anger was at him, a lot of it was *your own* stuff. And *none* of the anger should have come out in the form of a beating.

9. It was *your* responsibility to make your home child-proof.

10. It was *your* responsibility to find support—babysitters, friends, and others to watch your son when you needed a break.

11. Counseling could have helped you lower your stress.

12. It was *your* responsibility to teach him, in a loving way, what "No!" means, and what to stay away from.

13. It was *your* responsibility to watch after him and discipline him *lovingly— not* brutally.

Skill #7: Drop the grudge.
You don't have any grudges to drop. You have only guilt and, possibly, remorse. The section on "Grieving" may help. Counseling may help.

Now you can take the time to learn the skills, and get the help, you needed earlier. If your son is physically disabled, you can use the skills to be kind and loving to him. You also can *get*—and then *support*—all the help available to him.

If your son is brain-damaged, you still need the skills to be kind and loving to him. People who have trouble thinking or understanding *still have feelings.*

If your son is dead, you can learn to be kinder to the people who are left in your life.

The section on "Grieving" will help in any case.

Grief

When my grandmother died, I was so sad I couldn't even cry. I was 12 years old.

She was the one who really raised me. She lived with me and my mother and my older sisters and brothers. But my mother worked, and when she was home she was always yelling at one of us. Everybody else was busy doing stuff, and Grandma was the only one I could talk to.

She'd read to me and tell me stories about when she was a little girl. When I got older and started my period, it was Grandma who told me about sex. Even when I had my first boyfriend and I wanted to hide everything from my mother, I told Grandma. I loved her, and I knew she loved me.

I was shocked at my own reaction when she died. I couldn't cry, not for a long time. But I got mad—angry at her for dying! How could she do this to me? I even felt ashamed for being angry. I thought how selfish I was, worrying about myself when Grandma's the one who died. But I was angry for days.

Finally, I broke down and cried. Cried and cried. Sad as I was, it felt better than being angry at her.

In this case:

Skill #1: Decide (1) if *you're* ready to talk about it, and (2) if the other person is ready.
Skill #1 doesn't work here. The anger is really inside you, not towards your grandmother. But some of the skills can help you deal with your loss.

Skill #2: Talk to the person you're angry at (and keep everyone else out of it).
This skill can help, but not in the typical way. Here, it can be good for you to "talk" to your grandmother, even though she isn't physically there to hear you. Do it when you're in a private, quiet place.

Skill #3: Pay attention to their feelings (as well as your own).
This skill also can help, in a non-typical way. You can think about your grandmother and imagine what she felt, as she read to you, listened to you, and talked with you.

Skill #4: Find something in common.
You know that you and your grandmother loved each other.

Skill #5: Depersonalize the situation.
Her death was not "aimed" at you. It is a very personal loss. But it wasn't "about" you.

Skill #6: Get to the *real* issue(s).
The real issues are:

1. Your sadness at losing your grandmother.

2. You are going through the grieving process.

3. The grieving process includes anger, along with other bad feelings.

4. It can take a while to get *to* the anger and sadness. There are steps in the grieving process. Each of us goes through the steps in our own way, at our own pace.

Skill #7: Drop the grudge.
You really don't have a grudge. You have a loss. You have the sadness that goes with it. You have the grieving process to go through, over time. The section on "Grieving" can help you.

Domestic violence

I'm more afraid of him than in love with him.

I probably loved him at the beginning. He was always so sweet to me when we were dating. He paid more attention to me than any guy ever had.

But slowly, just a little bit at a time, he started finding fault with me. I was too fat, or too short, or too loud. He'd always find something. When it hurt my feelings, he'd say he was just joking. When he yelled, it was clear that he really felt that way.

I can see it now, looking back. But I didn't see it then. One by one, he made me get rid of all my friends. Each time, he had a good reason— good in his mind, that is. I got so lost in each example that I didn't see what was happening until later. Two, maybe three, years after we were married, I had no friends left.

He'd already started hitting me by then. It was because I did something stupid. Or looked at him wrong. Or was too fat or ugly. Then he started hitting me because he "knew" I had another man. Ha! I was already like a prisoner in my own house by then. Who could go find another man? And feeling so bad about myself, what man would want me anyway?

Then he started in on my family. Again, one by one. This cousin didn't like him, so it was bad for me to see her. Then another cousin. Then he got to my sister and my brothers. The last was my own mother. I can't believe I did it, looking back. But one by one, I gave up everyone close to me, for him.

Sometimes, when he'd hit me, he would cry with me and swear he'd never do it again. I believed him. I was so stupid! I believed him every time, even though he always hit me again. I was so afraid of him that I never even asked what made him do it.

Other times, he be in a rage and blame me. He said he really didn't want to hit me, but he knew I was lying to him, so it was my fault. Every time he hit me, he had a different excuse.

Sometimes, he'd hit me so hard I'd get a black eye. Other times, he'd hit my head against the wall and I'd feel really dizzy for a long time. He yelled that I deserved this because of how cheap my clothes made me look.

I always said I was sorry. But he'd always hit me again.

Now he hits me every time something goes wrong. It might be something I did, or something he thinks I did. It might be something that has nothing to do with me.

And he doesn't promise anymore that it won't happen again. Instead, he says it's my fault and I deserve it. And he says he'll kill me if I even think about leaving him.

I'm angry at him for what he does to me. I'm also terrified of him. But I'm also angry at myself. How did I let this happen?

In this case:

Skill #1: Decide (1) if *you're* ready to talk about it, and (2) if the other person is ready.
You've been ready for a long time. But *he* never will be. The skills can still help *you.*

Skill #2: Talk to the person you're angry at (and keep everyone else out of it).
This won't work without Skill #1. In this case, you'll have to talk to "everyone" *but* him.

Skill #3: Pay attention to their feelings (as well as your own).
His feelings have been all that mattered so far. Now it's *your* turn, for *your* feelings.

Skill #4: Find something in common.
This won't work without Skill #1. In this case, you have to focus on *yourself.*

Skill #5: Depersonalize the situation.
He's been forcing you to *take* things personally that were really *his* problems. You have to start getting rid of the blame you—and he—have put on you. You have to start seeing that *he—not you—*caused the violence against you.

Skill #6: Get to the *real* issue(s).
You have many real issues:

1. You've been in an abusive relationship all this time. You've been a victim of domestic violence.

2. *He*—not you—caused the violence. No matter what you did or said, *he* is responsible for how he reacts. No matter what he feels, *he's* the one who failed to make a S-P-A-C-E between what he *felt* and what he *did.*

3. Religious women—and even women who are not religious—often believe that they're supposed to "submit" to their husband. *But scriptural statements about this assumed that the husband was kind to the wife!* Even the scripture does not want a woman—or anyone—to stay in relationships where they're being beaten.

4. He used you as a *scapegoat*. He took out—on *you*—all his frustrations in life. Much of his anger came from early in his life, long before he even met you. Even his anger from today was made worse by *his own problems*. He blamed you because he was too ashamed to admit he couldn't handle his own problems.

5. Even thought you're not "perfect," *no one* is. That's why responsible adults use the seven skills in this book to *talk things over* when they're angry. Because *he* couldn't deal with his anger like a grown-up, he made up excuses to blame you for his problems. But he was *wrong*.

6. You're very wise to see, looking back, how he slowly made you lose all the people who loved you. His reason was simple: if they knew how he was treating you, they would have rushed to your rescue. He would have "lost" his "prisoner." By getting them out of your life, he gained more and more control over you. He used his anger to tighten that control.

7. He did not love you. *Not* because you're not lovable—you *are*. The problem is with *him*. *He is not able to love*. It's because he's still a self-centered infant, emotionally. It's *not* because of *you*. Like all self-centered infants in adults' bodies, he knew how to *act* nice sometimes because it made you believe he loved you. But all he really wanted was your body for sex, for target practice, for an outlet for his infant-like rage. A self-centered infant in a man's body is *very* dangerous.

8. Maybe you were raised to believe that if you were a good person and a good woman, you'd be loved by a good man. Or maybe you grew up with so much abuse that you thought this man would be "different." Or maybe you thought abuse was "normal," and now you know better.

   But healthy, loving relationships work *only* if both people involved are responsible adults. When you're in love with a self-centered infant in a man's body, you will be *used* and *victimized*—which you were. And again, it *wasn't* because of *you*.

9. One way he—like *all* abusers—"tricked" you into blaming yourself was to pick on your weaknesses. We *all* have something we don't like about ourselves—weight, looks, and other things. By picking on your weaknesses, he got you to *focus* on them. He got you to *exaggerate*, in your own mind, how "bad" they were. He got

you to *talk yourself into* believing you were to "blame" for *his anger.* He got you to make a "willing victim" of yourself. But the *truth* is that you were a loving, *unknowing* victim. Like a kidnapper who talks a little girl into getting in his car, he took advantage of your love and innocence—for *his* purposes.

10. You meant well, and you did the best you knew how to do. Now you have more information. You see him for how he really is. Now it's time to get on with *your* life. You *must* start with the grieving process—grieving for all the beliefs you had that weren't true, for the time you spent with him, for all you've lost in both a practical sense and an emotional sense. The section on "Grieving" will help. So will counseling.

11. Because you're in danger around him, you *must* find a shelter, or friend, or relative you can stay with. This practical step is the key to *saving* your life. You *must* do this before you can start *rebuilding* your life. You really have no choice—*unless* you leave *now*, you may end up *dead* pretty soon.

12. To do this, you *must* get help. From a friend, relative, religious leader, counselor, or someone else you can trust. You may have to go to a women's shelter. It *must* be someone you feel *comfortable* with. And you *must* feel comfortable with how well they *listen* to you. You have to feel comfortable with both *what* they tell you and *how* they tell it to you.

13. Do *not* trust a counselor or religious leader *just because* they're a counselor or religious leader! Most of them are very helpful. But some individuals in both fields have inflicted a great deal of pain on the people they were supposed to help. Trust your gut reactions, feelings, thoughts, intuition, and judgment.

14. *Avoid* sex counselors. They will focus on physical body parts, but will *not* be able to help you with your feelings.

15. See the section "How to Interview a Therapist or Helper" below.

Skill #7: Drop the grudge.
You've got to drop *him,* not just the grudge. The section on "How to Drop the Grudge So You Can Act *Now*" will help you take the steps to leave. The section on "How to Drop the Grudge When the Other Person Wants

to *Get* You" will help you see him more clearly. The section on "Letting Go of Grudges in General" will help broaden your view. And the section on "Grieving" will help you resolve the past and move towards the future.

How to Interview a Therapist or Helper

This is about trusting *your own judgment, intuition, feelings, knowledge*—and yourself in general. Counselors, religious leaders, and other therapists can *help* you—but they *also* can *hurt* you. This checklist will help you make sure you're safe with your "helper"! *Even this checklist is just a guideline—add your own items, and use your own judgment.* *Before* you start telling them too much, ask yourself:

1. How *comfortable* do you feel *with* them—and *about* them?

2. How much do they *talk* to you—versus *listen* to you?

3. How much do they *"put answers in your mouth"*—versus *really* hear you?

4. How much do they emphasize *sex*—versus the *abuse and power problems* in your life?

5. How much do they *push* their own views, values, and issues on you—versus *listen* to *yours*?

6. How much do they talk as if *there is no right or wrong, and no normal or abnormal*—versus emphasizing that the abuser is *wrong* to beat you, no matter "why" he does it, or how bad his childhood was?

7. How much do they tell you they can "fix everything"—versus the fact that *all they can do is help you get back on your feet*?

8. How much do they "string out" the *length of time the therapy will take*—versus telling you, up front, that the process will take *somewhere between several weeks and a couple of months*?

9. How much do they say *they can make you better*—versus *emphasize that they can help* YOU *take charge of your life*?

10. What do *your gut, intuition, feelings, and thoughts* tell you? *Trust* them to tell you whether or not this is the right person to help you. Feelings of "alarm" may be *small*—but they're extremely *important* to follow.

11. Add *your own* rules to this checklist.

12. Trust your gut feelings.

Giving up addictions

I knew for a long time that I smoked and drank too much. Did drugs too much. I even quit a few times. But not for long.

At first, it felt so powerful to quit. Every time. Like I was on top of things, I could handle it. Kind of like a high in itself.

And fighting the urge, that felt powerful too. Even the headaches and the sleepless nights felt like just a test at first. A challenge.

But here's what got me every time. My moods. I got real moody, real sensitive, every time I quit. Everyone got on my nerves. Everything they did bothered me.

I got angry real easy. And real fast. I even got afraid of my anger. I wanted to tell everybody off. I wanted to hit them, beat them up. I got angry at anything anyone did or said. I yelled a lot.

I was shocked. This wasn't like me. I never got this way when I smoked or did drugs or drank. I was afraid of myself. I was afraid of my own anger. I was afraid of what I might do.

It was easier to go back to smoking, drinking, drugging.

In this case:

Skill #1: Decide (1) if *you're* ready to talk about it, and (2) if the other person is ready.
This is between you and *yourself*—not another person.

Skill #2: Talk to the person you're angry at (and keep everyone else out of it).
You don't need this skill in this case.

Skill #3: Pay attention to their feelings (as well as your own).
It's *your* feelings that matter here.

Skill #4: Find something in common.
You don't need this skill in this case.

Skill #5: Depersonalize.

You've already depersonalized *too much*. You're using drugs, alcohol, and nicotine to *get away* from yourself—when you really need to get *closer* to who you are.

Skill #6: Get to the *real* issue(s).

You have several real issues:

1. You're *addicted* to nicotine, alcohol, and whatever drugs you use. Addiction means:

    a) What you're doing (smoking, drinking, doping, or any other activity that fits this definition) is *bad* for you—*physically, emotionally, mentally, and/or financially.*

    b) You *think* you can quit by yourself—but in reality, you *can't.*

    c) Your addiction *replaces* healthy relationships.

2. Part (a) means your substances are hurting your body, mind, and feelings. Not only your heart, lungs, immune system, and overall health, but *also* your physical *brain.* Short-term damage makes you lose control of your behavior, emotionally disconnect from those you love, get sick, and feel exhausted. Long-term damage ruins your judgment, behaviors, ability to feel, and your relationships. You spend your money on *substances*—instead of food, rent, your kids, your health, your future.

3. Part (b) means you need help. Treatment centers, 12-step programs, counseling, and other resources can help. But *only* if you *want* to quit. And *only* if you *go* for help. Your bad behaviors when you *quit* are *withdrawal* symptoms. You have to get past them, to get back to your real life.

4. Part (c) means that emotionally, you turn into an *infant* in a woman's body. Just like male abusers, who are infants in men's bodies!

    Addictions take away your adult maturity, experience, judgment, intelligence, and feelings for others. Addictions turn you back into an infant— totally wrapped up *only* in yourself, your own needs, and the *moment.*

    You're overrun with your *feelings*, just like infants are. You can't make a S-P-A-C-E between what you *feel* and what you *do*—just like infants can't. You—and everyone around you—are at the mercy of whatever *substance* you take, and whatever *mood* or *impulse* you feel, because you've lost control of yourself.

Your life becomes *chaos*. You lose your sense of yourself as a person. You lose your connection to other people. Your life *stops* when you're into addictions.

5. When you quit—with help, not by yourself—you will go through all the feelings you've tried to block out with addictions. For this reason, the section on "Grieving" will help you. All your bad feelings have gotten stuck inside you. The addictions let you block them out—for a while. Then, the feelings come back in force—and again, you use addictions to hide from them. Addictions are not about life. They're about hiding—and they're about death.

    The only way you can heal is to feel the feelings, through grieving. You can't do it alone because it's too hard. But with help, you can.

    And, with help, you can get your life back.

Skill #7: Drop the grudge.
You probably have a lot of grudges towards different people, for different reasons. You may not even remember all of them, because of hiding behind your addictions. But they will come out in your grieving process. That's part of your healing.

The section on "Letting Go of Grudges in General" will help, along with the "Grieving" section.

Your real choice *now* is between your addictions and your life.

Incest

My father started molesting me when I was about four. He'd do it while my mother was out doing her friends' hair and he was supposed to be babysitting me. He'd bring me to his bed and fondle me. I don't remember everything he did to me.

When I turned 12 and got my period, I told him to stop or I'd tell my mother on him. It took me all those years before I had the guts to say that to him. He stopped.

I can't believe my mother didn't know. I can't believe she didn't see how I couldn't look her in the eye. How I didn't want to be near him at all. How I cried when she left to do her friends' hair. When I was little, I thought she could tell how I felt inside. I felt sick, scared, and angry. I felt ashamed. I felt guilty. I felt very, very alone. I felt afraid of my own father.

It took me a few years to tell her about it. I was 15. She asked why I was so rude to him. Why I refused to go anywhere with the two of them. So I told her.

At first, she didn't believe me. That made me furious. But I felt too guilty and ashamed, maybe even afraid, to get mad at her. I just kept telling her the same thing, over and over.

Finally, one day, she said she believed me. I started to feel this immense relief all over my body. I felt like a big sigh of relief was finally coming out of me. I felt like she would do something to make it right. Get him arrested. Divorce him. Make him see how he'd hurt me. And her.

Instead, she was real quiet for a while. Then she said, "I believe you. I'm sorry he did that to you. But he's your father. He's the breadwinner. Just be nice to him, and I'll make sure you're not alone with him anymore."

I left home as soon as I could. I married this jerk, just to get out of the house. I didn't know how to work or do anything like that. I couldn't leave on my own.

On the outside, it looks like everything's fine with me. I have kids. I'm still married. I look okay.

But nothing changed inside me. I still can't stand to be touched. I hold my breath and stare at the ceiling every time we have sex. I can barely hug my own kids. The only good thing I've done for my kids is keep them away from my father. I say and do all the right things. But I don't feel like I'm alive anymore.

I'm angry at my father for what he did. My mother thinks she's supportive of me, because she believes me. But she can't see that I'm angry at her, too—for not doing anything about the truth. Even today, she's glad I act like nothing happened.

As angry as I am at my father, I'm much angrier at my mother.

In this case:

Skill #1: Decide (1) if *you're* ready to talk about it, and (2) if the other person is ready.
You were very brave to talk to your mother in the first place. Of course it took a long time—you were young. But the fact that you told her means you probably are ready to talk to her again. This time, about your anger at *her.*

She did finally listen to you when you told her. You should try again now. She may be ready, as well.

Skill #2: Talk to the person you're angry at (and keep everyone else out of it).
For now, keep this between you and your mother. *She's* the one you're most angry at now.

Skill #3: Pay attention to their feelings (as well as your own).
Unfair as it may seem, she'll be more likely to hear you *if* you say something about how *she* feels. You can start with something like, "I know this may upset you," or "I know you think everything is okay with me, but...," or something else that mentions *her* feelings.

When you pay attention to her feelings, you'll have a better chance of getting her to listen to *your* feelings.

Skill #4: Find something in common.
You're mother and daughter. You both want *you* to feel better. You both want things to *be* better.

Skill #5: Depersonalize the situation.
One of the bad things about incest—and child molestation in general—is that you, the victim, are likely to blame yourself. Not only for your father's molestation of you, but also for your mother's bad feelings.

It's natural to feel these ways. But it's important to remember that *you* are the *victim.* Your father is the abuser. Your mother is his accomplice—his helper—by failing to *do* anything about it.

They both hurt *you.* It was *their* fault—*not yours.*

Skill #6: Get to the *real* issue(s).
You have a number of real issues:

1. Your father used Self-Centered Anger, Two-Faced Anger, and Rigid Anger against you. He also used *denial.*

2.   Your mother used Self-Centered Anger and Two-Faced Anger. She also has been using tremendous amounts of *denial.*

3.   Your father molesting you—*and* doing it *regularly* for *so many years*—has hurt you emotionally, psychologically, and mentally, as well as physically. You have every *right* to be angry. Your anger is *justified.*

4.   Your mother's *failure* to do anything about it has "added insult to injury." It makes you feel like you *don't matter,* are *not important,* are *not worth caring about.* Her *lack* of action hurts you emotionally, psychologically, and mentally—just as her *failure to protect you* hurt you physically. Your anger is *justified.*

5.   You need to tell your mother you're angry at her, and why. You need to give her *your side of it.* What it was like. How you felt. How you felt about your father. How you felt about yourself. How you feel about her. This has to come *out*—and she has to *listen.*

6.   *Do not* let her interrupt you with practical details! For example, she's likely to interrupt you by saying, "Well, if he was arrested and in jail, we wouldn't have a roof over our heads." The *practical* side—and your mother's *reasons* for doing nothing—are *not* important *here. This* part of the conversation is for *you* to get your *feelings* out—and for her to *listen.*

7.   *Do not* let *yourself* be stopped by practical details! Again, this can be talked about later. But also, the truth is that even if she couldn't have gotten help from family members, there are community services that could have helped. No matter what your mother thought—or what she says now—you and she would *not* have gone "without a roof over your heads" if she'd reported him to the police.

8.   Your mother had her *own* personal issues and reasons for *"not noticing"* and *not doing anything* when you told her. These are *her* problems—*not yours.* You did *not* cause them. You were *victimized by* them.

9.   You did *not* cause the molestation. Your father is *sick.* He needed help, but did *not* get any. Instead, he took his sickness out on *you.* By doing *nothing* about it, your mother "helped" him stay sick.

10. Counseling would be very helpful to you. Your father and mother need counseling also, but that's *their* issue. *Your* issue is to take good care of *yourself.*

Skill #7: Drop the grudge.
The section on "Grieving" will help. So will the sections on "How to Drop the Grudge When the Other Person Wants to *Get* You," and "Letting Go of Grudges in General."

The section on "How to Drop the Grudge So You Can Act *Now*" will help you get ready to talk to your mother.

Pornography

My husband is always looking at porn magazines and videos, plus the computer, of course. The worst part is, he wants these videos on, and the pictures around, when we have sex.

It makes me angry. Aren't I good enough? Why should I have to compete with all these knockout models? It may turn him on more, but it turns me off. It feels like a real put-down to me. Like a reminder that I'm really nothing special. The more turned on these models make him, the more I feel like just the handy local place he can plug himself in!

Lately, he complains that he can't get turned on without this stuff. He says it's my fault. He says if I lost weight and went to the gym, he wouldn't have this problem.

And I could lose a few pounds, all right. But there's something about this whole thing that makes me really mad.

* * * *

I know that men like these girlie magazines and videos and stuff, but my boyfriend is so far into this that it makes me furious. What he likes seems really sick to me—scenes that look like the woman is ready for her gynecologist to give her an exam, and scenes that look disgusting instead of sexy.

There's even some that have kids in them! That's sick. But the worst is ones that show people getting cut and hurt. That's not about sex—it's about torture.

I get so sick to my stomach that it makes me angry. What does this say about my boyfriend? What kind of guy is he, anyway? Am I even safe with him? Are my kids? Does he really see us as a woman and kids—or as toys or future victims?

If he gets off on stuff that makes me sick and afraid, how can I trust him with us? That makes me furious!

In these cases:

Skill #1: Decide (1) if *you're* ready to talk about it, and (2) if the other person is ready.
You're *very* ready. Assume he is, as well. In both cases, your sense of him—and your relationship with him—depend on getting your issues out in the open. You may not like what you learn. But you're better off knowing—and then making more decisions about *him*.

Skill #2: Talk to the person you're angry at (and keep everyone else out of it).
Keep this between you and him. Everyone has different opinions. All that matters are yours and his.

Skill #3: Pay attention to their feelings (as well as your own).
It will help to start out by saying that you know he likes porn. Give him this, to help make it easier for him to hear what you have to say about *your* feelings.

Skill #4: Find something in common.
You have your relationship in common. You have your sexual relationship—at least, the part *you're* involved in—in common, as well.

Skill #5: Depersonalize the situation.
This is hard to believe—but the porn is *not* about *you*. Even if you were a porn star, he'd still have to see *other* porn. In some ways, it's a lot like addiction. But the point here is that his interest in porn has *nothing* to do with any "*shortcoming*" or "problem" with *you*.

Skill #6: Get to the *real* issue(s).
You have several real issues here:

1. He's using Drinking/Drugging Anger—with porn, instead of alcohol or drugs, as his addiction. He's also using Self-Centered Anger, Two-Faced Anger, and Rigid Anger on you.

2. The fact that something he's doing bothers you *should* matter to him. When the "something" relates to sex, this should matter *more* to him—*if* he cares about you.

3. With "plain" porn, he's using women as *toys, objects,* and *things*—not as *people*. It's one way he *looks down on* women. To him, women are *nothing*. His interest in porn shows intense *anger* towards women.

4. With "plain" porn, you *feel* second-best—or worse! You feel like these women "show you up" and you're "not good enough." His interest in porn feels like a *put-down* to *you*. Like a *power-play*.

5. With "plain" porn, you feel "blocked out," as if he's put a *barrier* between himself and you. The same way being drunk, or being loaded, can create a block between two people.

6. With child porn and with sadistic porn, he's showing even more *anger—and hatred—*towards women and life itself. He shows a huge need for *revenge, power,* and *control.* If these are his "fantasies," what does this tell you about him—or your interest in being with him?

7. How *willing* is he to talk about this with you? The more open and willing he is, the more likely he will really hear you and understand how you feel.

8. The *less willing* he is to talk about it, the less you *matter* to him and the less able he is to relate to you as an adult.

9. Besides the porn itself, you have more questions to ask yourself.

    ■ How much does he *really* relate to you, versus how much does he *prefer* the escape of fantasy?

    ■ How do you *feel about*—and what do you *think of*—the "fantasies" he enjoys?

    ■ What does this *say* about his ability to care about *people*?

    ■ What does it say about his ability to make a S-P-A-C-E between what he *feels* and what he *does*?

    ■ What does it say about his feelings for *you?*

    ■ How do his fantasies—and what they say about *him*—fit into your life together?

10. *You* have to decide whether you are even *safe* with him—much less *loved* by him.

11. If the discussion is rough, or if you don't like the answers, counseling might help. For him, for both of you—or for you alone. To help figure out what you want to do.

Skill #7: Drop the grudge.

Whatever the outcome, the section on "How to Drop the Grudge When the Other Person Wants to *Get* You" will help you take steps you need to take. The section on "Letting Go of Grudges in General" will help. So will the section on "Grieving."

* * * * *

Putting You—Not Anger—in Control of Your Life

There are a lot of people out there who will try to control you with their anger. And sometimes even your *own* anger takes over your life.

Now you know how to make a S-P-A-C-E between what you *feel* and what you *do*.

You have read about the seven ways other people can get you angry or control you by their own anger: Acted-Out Anger, Irresponsible Anger, Self-Centered Anger, Two-Faced Anger, Rigid Anger, Drinking/Drugging Anger, and Delusional Anger.

And you now have seven skills you can use that help you to react in ways that are *different* from what they expect or want, and thus prevent them—and your anger—from getting control over you:

1.   *Decide* if you—and they—are ready to talk

2.   Talk *only* to the person you're angry at

3.   Pay attention to *their* feelings

4.   Find something in *common*

5.   Depersonalize the situation

6.   Get to the real issue(s)

7.   Drop the grudge

It's *your* life. You can stop letting *other people's* anger run it for you. And you can stop letting *your own* anger run it for you. You can stop letting *anyone's* anger control your life. It's *your* turn. Now *you* are in charge of your life.

The Author

Lynne McClure, Ph.D., is a nationally recognized expert in managing high-risk behavior. President of McClure Associates, Inc., in the Phoenix area, Dr. McClure is also the author of *Angry Women: Stop Letting Anger Control Your Life, Anger & Conflict in the Workplace: Spot the Signs, Avoid the Trauma,* and *Risky Business: Managing Employee Violence in the Workplace,* and *Managing High-Risk Behaviors* (video). Dr. McClure has been featured by *CNN News Stand, CBS This Morning, The O'Reilly Factor,* and other prominent media. Clients include Fortune 500 companies and government agencies. The firm's website is www.McClureAssociates.com.

Index

A

Abuse:
    child, 99-101
    issue of, 82-83, 106, 108
    spousal, 104
Accusation, 55, 57, 98
Addiction, 15, 69, 78, 109-111, 116
Alcohol, 32, 34, 90, 109, 116
Anger:
    acted-out, 25-27, 93, 100, 118
    delusional, 33-35, 118
    drinking/drugging, 32-33, 77, 93,
        116, 118
    irresponsible, 27-28, 100, 118
    other people's, 20, 25-35
    rigid, 31-32, 82, 86, 89, 91, 93,
        100, 113, 116, 118
    self-centered, 28-29, 77, 85, 96,
        100, 113, 114, 116, 118
    two-faced, 29-31, 77, 82, 86, 98,
        100, 113, 114, 116, 118
Anorexia, 7, 21, 80-83
Apologize, 56
Arrest, 86-87
Attack, 65
Attacker, 90, 91

B-C

Body language, 45-47
Boss, 11, 21, 55, 56, 94, 97-99
Boyfriend, 8, 11, 17, 42, 55, 56, 57,
    59, 60, 77, 84-87, 102, 115

Change, 56, 57
Children, 22, 25, 76, 99-101
Co-worker, 84, 98

Control:
    lack of, 7, 80, 94, 99-101, 111
    of women, 23, 25-27, 29, 31, 33,
        41, 51, 57, 62, 63, 64, 68-
        69, 71, 72-73, 78, 82, 86, 87,
        89, 90, 91, 92, 106, 117, 118
Counseling, 78-79, 82, 86-87, 90, 91,
    96, 101, 107, 110, 114, 117
Counselor, 83, 85, 91, 107, 108
Court, 91
Crime, 90

D-F

Date-rape, 9, 88-91
Death, 13, 72
Defensive, 44, 45, 46, 51, 98
Delusion, 33-35
Denial, 68, 72, 78, 113, 114
Dependence, 31, 78
Depersonalize, 53-57, 59, 67, 71, 73,
    81, 85, 89, 93, 96, 97, 100, 103,
    105, 110, 113, 116, 118
Depression, 70, 90, 94
Drugged, 88-89
Drugs, 15, 32, 34, 68, 88, 89, 90, 93-
    94, 109-110, 116

Eating, 2, 7, 80, 82
Eating disorder therapists, 82

Fantasy, 117
Fatigue, chronic, 2
Fault, 41, 44, 72, 82, 113
Fear, 1, 9, 31, 70, 88
FEELDO, 20, 21, 22, 25, 101

Feelings, 23, 25, 27, 29, 30, 31, 44-47, 49, 50, 51, 55, 59, 67, 70, 72, 73, 77, 78, 81, 83, 85, 89, 90, 93, 95, 97, 100-101, 102, 104, 105, 109, 110, 111, 113, 116, 117, 118
Food, 7, 80-81, 83

G-H
Get even, 56
Grief, 13, 72-73, 102-103
Grieving, 87, 91, 94, 96, 101, 103, 107-108, 111, 115, 118
Grudge, 67-73, 79, 83, 87, 90, 91, 94, 96, 99, 101, 103, 107-108, 111, 115, 118
Guilt, 70, 101
Guilty, 76

Hallucination, 33-35
Happy, 70
Harassment, 65
Harm, physical, 12, 21, 114
Healing, 69-70, 71, 72
Helper, 107-109
Hepatitis C, 94
Human resources, 65, 87
Hurt, 1, 3, 17, 20, 54, 69, 71, 93, 108, 110, 114
Husband, 59, 60, 76-79, 104-108, 115

I-L
Incest, 16, 112-115
Independent, 1, 78-79, 86-87, 94
Innocence, 91, 107
Issue:
    real, 59-65, 67, 71, 73, 77, 82-83, 85, 89, 93-94, 96, 98, 100-101, 103, 105-107, 110-111, 113-114, 116-118
    work performance, 98

Jealousy, 6, 76
Job, 11, 72, 94, 97
Justice, 91

Kids, 6, 12, 21, 22, 59, 60, 76, 99-101, 112, 115

Legal system, 91
Letting go, 67

M-Q
Men, 1, 2, 33
Misinterpret, 56
Misunderstanding, 63
Molestation, 7, 16, 80, 82, 83, 93, 112, 113, 114

Nothing to lose, 68

Parties, 88
Passive, 1
Perpetrator, 91
Planning, 78
Police, 65, 90, 91, 114
Pornography, 17, 115-118
Post-traumatic stress, 90
Power, 31, 117
Power-play, 117
Predator, 89
Prostitution, 10, 92
Put down, 2, 29, 63, 71, 117

Questioning, 8, 33, 84-86, 97

R-S
Rape, 9, 88-91
Rapist, 89-90
Relationship, 83, 85, 87, 105, 106, 110, 116
Remorse, 101
Responsibility, 27, 28, 93, 101

Restraining orders, 86-87
Revenge, 117

Sadness, 70, 103
Security, 87
Self-defense, 70
Self-destructive, 90, 93
Self-respect, 32
Self-righteous, 68
Sex, 6, 8, 16, 17, 84, 102, 106, 108, 112, 115, 116
Sexy, 76, 115
Shelter, women's, 107
Shock, 72-73
Shoplifting, 11, 28, 95
Social service agencies, 94
Sodomize, 9, 88, 90
Something in common, 50-51, 57, 59, 67, 73, 77, 81, 85, 89, 93, 96, 97, 100, 103, 105, 109, 113, 116, 118
Something to gain, 68
S-P-A-C-E, 20-34, 37, 53, 63, 64, 71, 100, 101, 105, 110, 117, 118
Stealing, 94, 96
Stress, 1, 101,
Suicide, 2, 3, 90
Suspects, 91
Symptoms, 60, 61, 62, 82

T-W
Take charge, 20-24
Talk, 37-38, 40-42, 44-47, 51, 55, 62, 64, 67, 73, 77, 81, 82, 85, 89, 93, 95, 97, 99-100, 102, 105, 109, 113, 116, 118
Therapist, 107-109
Therapy, 108
Training, 94
Treatment centers, 78, 94, 110
Trust, 81, 91, 115
Twelve-step programs, 78, 94, 110

Unfairness, 11, 97

Valium, 6, 21, 76-78
Victim, 107, 113, 114
Violence, domestic, 14, 104-108

Weaknesses, 106
Withdrawal, 69, 110
Witnesses, 91,
Work, 11, 98-99

Career Resources

The following Career Resources are available directly from Impact Publications. Full descriptions of each title as well as nine downloadable catalogs, videos, and software can be found on our website: www.impact publications.com. Complete the following form or list the titles, include shipping (see formula at the end), enclose payment, and send your order to:

IMPACT PUBLICATIONS
9104 Manassas Drive, Suite N
Manassas Park, VA 20111-5211 USA
1-800-361-1055 (orders only)
Tel. 703-361-7300 or Fax 703-335-9486
Email address: info@impactpublications.com
Quick & easy online ordering: www.impactpublications.com

Orders from individuals must be prepaid by check, money order, or major credit card. We accept telephone, fax, and email orders.

Qty.	TITLES	Price	TOTAL
Books and Videos By Author			
_____	Angry Anger and Conflict in the Workplace	$15.95	_____
_____	Angry Men	14.95	_____
_____	Angry Women	14.95	_____
_____	Managing High-Risk Behaviors Video	149.95	_____
Anger and Conflict Books			
_____	Anger Busting	$14.95	_____
_____	Anger-Free	12.00	_____
_____	Angry All the Time	13.95	_____
_____	Beyond Anger: A Guide for Men	14.95	_____
_____	Controlling People	12.95	_____
_____	Emotionally Abused Women	13.50	_____
_____	On Killing	15.95	_____
_____	Overcoming Anger and Irritability	14.95	_____
_____	Transforming Anger	10.95	_____
_____	Verbally Abusive Relationship	10.95	_____
_____	You Can't Say That To Me	18.95	_____

Anger and Conflict Videos

_____ Assertive Communication Skills	$149.95	_____
_____ Best 10 1/4 Tips for Controlling Anger	98.00	_____
_____ Cage the Rage: Handling Your Anger	89.00	_____
_____ Dealing With Conflict and Confrontation	199.95	_____
_____ How to Handle Conflict	149.95	_____
_____ Managing High-Risk Behaviors	149.00	_____

College-to-Career Resources

_____ 200 Best Jobs for College Graduates	$16.95	_____
_____ America's Top Jobs for College Graduates	15.95	_____
_____ Best Resumes for College Students and New Grads	12.95	_____
_____ College Majors Handbook	24.95	_____
_____ Great Careers in Two Years	19.95	_____
_____ The Job Hunting Guide	14.95	_____
_____ Quick Guide to College Majors and Careers	16.95	_____

Testing and Assessment

_____ Career Tests	$12.95	_____
_____ Discover the Best Jobs for You	15.95	_____
_____ Discover What You're Best At	14.00	_____
_____ Do What You Are	18.95	_____
_____ I Don't Know What I Want, But I Know It's Not This	14.00	_____
_____ Pathfinder	14.00	_____
_____ Seven Habits of Highly Effective People	14.00	_____
_____ What Should I Do With My Life?	24.95	_____
_____ What's Your Type of Career?	18.95	_____
_____ What Type Am I?	14.95	_____
_____ Who Moved My Cheese?	19.95	_____

Inspiration and Empowerment

_____ Life Strategies	$13.95	_____
_____ Maximum Success	24.95	_____
_____ Seven Habits of Highly Effective People	14.00	_____
_____ Who Moved My Cheese?	19.95	_____

Career Exploration and Job Strategies

_____ 25 Jobs That Have It All	$12.95	_____
_____ 300 Best Jobs Without a Four–Year Degree	16.95	_____
_____ Almanac of American Employers	199.95	_____
_____ America's Top 100 Jobs for People Without a Four-Year Degree	19.95	_____
_____ Directory of Executive Recruiters	49.95	_____
_____ Occupational Outlook Handbook	18.95	_____
_____ The O*NET Guide	38.95	_____
_____ Quick Guide to Career Training in Two Years or Less	16.95	_____
_____ Quick Prep Careers	18.95	_____
_____ Quit Your Job and Grow Some Hair	15.95	_____

_____ 50 Cutting Edge Jobs	$15.95	_____
_____ 95 Mistakes Job Seekers Make	13.95	_____
_____ 100 Great Jobs and How to Get Them	17.95	_____
_____ Best Jobs for the 21st Century	19.95	_____
_____ Best Keywords for Resumes, Cover Letters, Interviews	17.95	_____
_____ Change Your Job, Change Your Life (8th Edition)	17.95	_____
_____ Internships	26.95	_____
_____ No One Will Hire Me!	13.95	_____
_____ Occupational Outlook Handbook	16.95	_____
_____ What Color Is Your Parachute?	17.95	_____

Internet Job Search

_____ America's Top Internet Job Sites	$19.95	_____
_____ CareerXroads (annual)	26.95	_____
_____ e-Resumes	11.95	_____
_____ Haldane's Best Employment Websites for Professionals	15.95	_____

Resumes and Letters

_____ 101 Quick Tips for a Dynamite Resume	$13.95	_____
_____ 201 Dynamite Job Search Letters	19.95	_____
_____ Best Cover Letters for $100,000+ Jobs	24.95	_____
_____ Best KeyWords for Resumes, Cover Letters, and Interviews	17.95	_____
_____ Best Resumes and CVs for International Jobs	24.95	_____
_____ Best Resumes for $100,000+ Jobs	24.95	_____
_____ Best Resumes for People Without a Four-Year Degree	19.95	_____
_____ Cover Letters for Dummies	16.99	_____
_____ Dynamite Cover Letters (4th Edition)	14.95	_____
_____ Dynamite Resumes (4th Edition)	14.95	_____
_____ e-Resumes	11.95	_____
_____ Expert Resumes for People Returning to Work	16.95	_____
_____ Haldane's Best Cover Letters for Professionals	15.95	_____
_____ Haldane's Best Resumes for Professionals	15.95	_____
_____ High Impact Resumes and Letters (8th Edition)	19.95	_____
_____ Resumes in Cyberspace	14.95	_____
_____ Resumes for Dummies	16.99	_____
_____ Resumes That Knock 'Em Dead	12.95	_____
_____ The Savvy Resume Writer	12.95	_____
_____ Sure-Hire Resumes	14.95	_____

Networking

_____ A Foot in the Door	$14.95	_____
_____ How to Work a Room	14.00	_____
_____ Masters of Networking	16.95	_____
_____ The Savvy Networker	13.95	_____

Dress, Image, and Etiquette

_____	Dressing Smart for Men	$16.95 _____
_____	Dressing Smart for Women	16.95 _____
_____	Dressing Smart for the New Millennium	15.95 _____

Interviews and Salary Negotiations

_____	101 Dynamite Questions to Ask At Your Job Interview	$13.95 _____
_____	Dynamite Salary Negotiations	15.95 _____
_____	Haldane's Best Answers to Tough Interview Questions	15.95 _____
_____	Haldane's Best Salary Tips for Professionals	15.95 _____
_____	Interview for Success (8th Edition)	15.95 _____
_____	Job Interviews for Dummies	16.99 _____
_____	Job Interview Tips for People With Not-So-Hot Backgrounds	13.95 _____
_____	KeyWords to Nail Your Job Interview	17.95 _____
_____	Nail the Job Interview!	13.95 _____
_____	The Savvy Interviewer	10.95 _____

Government, International, and Nonprofit

_____	Book of U.S. Government Jobs	$21.95 _____
_____	Directory of Websites for International Jobs	19.95 _____
_____	Electronic Federal Resume Guidebook, with CD-ROM	44.95 _____
_____	Federal Applications That Get Results	23.95 _____
_____	Federal Resume Guidebook (3rd Edition)	21.95 _____
_____	FBI Careers	18.95 _____
_____	Find a Federal Job Fast!	15.95 _____
_____	Global Citizen	16.95 _____
_____	Going Global Career Guide	199.95 _____
_____	Inside Secrets to Finding a Job in Travel	14.95 _____
_____	International Job Finder	19.95 _____
_____	International Jobs	18.00 _____
_____	Jobs and Careers With Nonprofit Organizations	17.95 _____
_____	Jobs for Travel Lovers	19.95 _____
_____	Post Office Jobs	17.95 _____
_____	Ten Steps to a Federal Job	39.95 _____

SUBTOTAL   _____

Virginia residents add 4½% sales tax   _____

POSTAGE/HANDLING ($5 for first
product and 8% of SUBTOTAL)   _____

8% of SUBTOTAL $5.00

TOTAL ENCLOSED   _____

SHIP TO:

NAME _____

ADDRESS _____

_____

_____

PAYMENT METHOD:

❑ I enclose check/money order for $ _____ made payable to
IMPACT PUBLICATIONS.

❑ Please charge $ _____ to my credit card:

❑ Visa ❑ MasterCard ❑ American Express ❑ Discover

Card # _____ Expiration date: ___ / ___

Signature _____

Keep in Touch . . .
On the Web!

www.impactpublications.com
www.ishoparoundtheworld.com
www.hoteltravelshop.com
www.mycruiseshop.com
www.contentfortravel.com
www.winningthejob.com
www.veteransworld.com
www.contentforcareers.com